Mastering SOLIDWORKS Sheet Metal

Enhance your 3D modeling skills by learning all aspects of the SOLIDWORKS Sheet Metal module

Johno Ellison

BIRMINGHAM—MUMBAI

Mastering SOLIDWORKS Sheet Metal

Copyright © 2022 Packt Publishing

All rights reserved. No part of this book may be reproduced, stored in a retrieval system, or transmitted in any form or by any means, without the prior written permission of the publisher, except in the case of brief quotations embedded in critical articles or reviews.

Every effort has been made in the preparation of this book to ensure the accuracy of the information presented. However, the information contained in this book is sold without warranty, either express or implied. Neither the author, nor Packt Publishing or its dealers and distributors, will be held liable for any damages caused or alleged to have been caused directly or indirectly by this book.

Packt Publishing has endeavoured to provide trademark information about all of the companies and products mentioned in this book by the appropriate use of capitals. However, Packt Publishing cannot guarantee the accuracy of this information.

Associate Group Product Manager: Rohit Rajkumar
Publishing Product Manager: Kaustubh Manglurkar
Senior Editor: Keagan Carneiro
Content Development Editor: Adrija Mitra
Technical Editor: Simran Udasi
Copy Editor: Safis Editing
Project Coordinator: Rashika Ba
Proofreader: Safis Editing
Indexer: Manju Arasan
Production Designer: Prashant Ghare
Marketing Coordinator: Elizabeth Varghese

First published: February 2022
Production reference: 2100222

Published by Packt Publishing Ltd.
Livery Place
35 Livery Street
Birmingham
B3 2PB, UK.

978-1-80324-524-9

www.packt.com

Contributors

About the author

Johno Ellison is a UK design engineer who has worked with SolidWorks 3D CAD since 2006. He has a wide range of product design and engineering experience, covering areas including mechanisms, 3D printing, materials selection, and rapid prototyping.

His online SolidWorks courses have been taken by hundreds of thousands of students and he has worked with over 300 clients from all around the world. He holds a first-class honors degree in Sustainable Product Design from a top 25 UK university and has completed a range of SolidWorks-certified training courses in the UK. He also holds two Guinness World Records (Longest Distance covered, and Highest Altitude reached), for driving a London Taxi.

I would to thank the entire team at Packt for helping to make this process go so smoothly, particularly Adrija for being such a great editor to work with, Kaustubh for overseeing the project, and Vaideeshwari Muralikrishnanfor for initially reaching out to me.
I'd also like to thank my wife, Lindsay, for listening to me bang on about K-factors, and for helping to make sure that everything made sense!

About the reviewer

Thomas P. McDunn is an automation engineer with experience in machine design, electronics, and software of all kinds. Tom holds bachelor's and master's degrees in mechanical engineering. He currently teaches classes and workshops in 3D CAD and 3D printing. He practices 3D design for 3D printing with eight of his own machines. He also uses 3D CAD design for CNC router projects. Thomas holds a patent for an industrial automation controller. He is passionate about computer control and robotics and volunteers at the local makerspace. He enjoys helping designers gain proficiency in CAD with his workshops and classes. Tom has worked with SolidWorks since the 1990s. He was a reviewer of the Packt Publication *Hands-On 3D Modeling with SolidWorks*.

Table of Contents

Section 2: Advanced Sheet Metal Tools

5

Creating Complex Parts Using Swept Flanges and the Fold/Unfold Tools

6

Utilizing Gussets, Cross Breaks, and Vents to Add Part Details

7

Producing Advanced Shapes Using Lofted Bends

8

Joining Multi-Sheet Parts Using Tab and Slot Features

9

Finishing Off Models Using Corner Details

10

Adding 3D Details to Models with Forming Tools

Section 3: Converting 3D Parts to Sheet Metal and Creating a Sheet Metal Enclosure

11

Converting to Sheet Metal Using the Insert Bends Tool

12

Building Sheet Metal Parts Using the Convert to Sheet Metal Tool

13

Practical Example: The Sheet Metal Enclosure

Index

Other Books You May Enjoy

Preface

SolidWorks is the premier software choice for 3D engineering and product design applications across a wide range of industries, and the Sheet Metal module makes up an important part of this powerful program.

This book will help you to understand exactly what sheet metal is, why it is used, and how you can make the most of this fundamental design technique. You'll start by understanding the foundations of the basic tools, including Base Flanges and Sketched Bends, before moving on to more complex features, such as Custom Forming Tools and Lofted Bends. The book covers all the necessary tools in a step-by-step manner and shares practical manufacturing tips and tricks that will allow you to apply the skills that you learn to real-world situations.

By the end of this book, you'll understand how to make the best use of the SolidWorks Sheet Metal tools and be able to create a whole range of 3D models and designs confidently.

Who this book is for

This book is for existing SolidWorks users who want to expand their skills and learn the specialist area of Sheet Metal design. This may be engineers looking to upskill, hobbyists wanting to expand their abilities, or simply modeling enthusiasts looking to enhance their skills and knowledge.

What this book covers

Chapter 1, *Sheet Metal Basics – Exploring Sheet Metal Properties and Material Selection*, outlines the various uses of sheet metal and how it can be used in SolidWorks. You will learn how to start a Sheet Metal part using the different Base Flange types, and how the Sheet Metal properties can be set and modified. A basic overview of material selection is also provided.

Chapter 2, Adding Bends Using Edge Flanges, explains how to turn a flat Base Flange into a 3D part by adding Edge Flanges – one of the most common building blocks of Sheet Metal parts. This chapter also explores the Edge Flange properties in more detail, including Flange Profiles, the use of multiple edges, and other details.

Chapter 3, Getting Familiar with Basic Tools in Sheet Metal, explains how to add and remove material using basic Sheet Metal tools, including Tabs, Cuts and Holes. New flange types such as the Miter Flange and Hem are also explained, as well Sketched Bends, which can be used to add more unusual bend styles. Finally, the Jog feature is explained, both from a theoretical and a practical perspective.

Chapter 4, Creating Sheet Metal Drawings and Exporting Files, explains how to create 2D drawings, which are essential if parts are to be manufactured and used in the real world, and shows how to create these and how to insert Flat Patterns, based on Sheet Metal parts. It also explains the various ways in which Sheet Metal parts can be exported for use, such as DXF and DWG file types.

Chapter 5, Creating Complex Parts Using Swept Flanges and the Fold/Unfold Tools, explains how and why Swept Flanges can be used. These flanges are similar to Miter Flanges but each has a specific use case. It also covers the folding and unfolding operations. These are distinct from flattening and unflattening and can be used to make specific features, such as cuts across bends.

Chapter 6, Utilizing Gussets, Crossbreaks, and Vents to Add Part Details, explains each feature in turn – how to use them and why and where they might be used. Vents are another common feature in Sheet Metal parts and are used for a wide variety of reasons, including to add cooling and access ports.

Chapter 7, Producing Advanced Shapes Using Lofted Bends, covers Lofted Bends, which are an advanced form of bend that can be used to create more complex shapes than standard flange types. There are two types of Lofted Bend Formed and Bent – and this chapter covers both, including the major differences between the two.

Chapter 8, Joining Multi-Sheet Parts Using Tab and Slot Features, covers The Tab and Slot tool, which can be used to simplify the joining of two Sheet Metal sheets by creating Tab and Slot features on each. This chapter explains how to use the basic tool, and covers the many sub-options in more detail.

Chapter 9, Finishing Off Models Using Corner Details, explains how SolidWorks Sheet Metal contains a number of specific corner tools that can be used to create many types of corner join, including closing corner gaps between flanges, adding welded corners, trimming away sharp edges, and adding corner relief around bend areas.

Chapter 10, Adding 3D Details to Models with Forming Tools, explains how to use existing Forming Tools from the SolidWorks Design Library, as well as how to modify Forming Tools and how to create and use entirely-Custom Forming Tools.

Chapter 11, Converting to Sheet Metal Using the Insert Bends Tool, covers how 3D models with a constant wall thickness, such as Shelled or Thin Feature parts can be converted into Sheet Metal parts by using the Insert Bends feature. This chapter shows how to use this option to create Sheet Metal parts.

Chapter 12, Building Sheet Metal Parts Using the Convert to Sheet Metal Tool, explains how the Convert to Sheet Metal tool can be used with 3D models that don't have a constant wall thickness. The tool is quite versatile and has a number of options that are explained in detail here.

Chapter 13, Practical Example: The Sheet Metal Enclosure, shows how to use various Sheet Metal techniques to create an example enclosure, while also providing handy tips and tricks for practical modeling.

To get the most out of this book

You should already have a basic level of SolidWorks knowledge and be able to use a Windows PC. It will be assumed that you already know the building blocks of 3D modeling, such as sketching, as well as creating and editing features.

For those of you who are completely new to SolidWorks, it is advisable to gain a firm foundation in solid modeling first before trying to use the Sheet Metal module covered in this book.

You should also have a SolidWorks license if you wish to practice the exercises and skills covered in the book.

Software/hardware covered in the book	Operating system requirements
SolidWorks	Windows

The examples given in this book were created using SolidWorks 2021. Different versions of SolidWorks can be used with the vast majority of the tools covered, but there may be minor differences in the interface and sub-options.

During the course of the book, if a certain tutorial or tool is causing problems, try double-checking all of the previous steps, or even try closing the part and starting again from the beginning.

Error messages in SolidWorks can be quite descriptive and often tell the user exactly what the issue is. So, if you're presented with an error, try to avoid the temptation to click **OK** *without reading it properly, and instead, attempt to carry out the action suggested in the message.*

If the problems persist, please feel free to contact me online via Twitter at `www.twitter.com/johnoellison`.

Throughout this book, millimeters are used as the unit of measurement, but this can be adjusted according to your preference by setting the model's units to inches (for example) and then typing the millimeter numerical value followed by mm *in the Smart Dimension tool when adding dimensions. This will automatically convert the millimeter values into inches (or your selected unit type).*

Download the color images

We also provide a PDF file that has color images of the screenshots and diagrams used in this book. You can download it here: `https://static.packt-cdn.com/downloads/9781803245249_ColorImages.pdf`.

Conventions used

There are a number of text conventions used throughout this book.

`Code in text`: Indicates code words in the text, database table names, folder names, filenames, file extensions, pathnames, dummy URLs, user input, and Twitter handles.

Here is an example: "This can be drawn using a Center Rectangle, `100x50mm` in size, and fixed to Origin."

Bold: Indicates a new term, an important word, or words that you see on screen. For instance, words in menus or dialog boxes appear in **bold**. Here is an example: "The **Edges Type** selection allows the corners of the tabs to either be Sharp, Filleted or Chamfered."

> **Tips or Important Notes**
> Appear like this.

Get in touch

Feedback from our readers is always welcome.

General feedback: If you have questions about any aspect of this book, email us at customercare@packtpub.com and mention the book title in the subject of your message.

Errata: Although we have taken every care to ensure the accuracy of our content, mistakes do happen. If you have found a mistake in this book, we would be grateful if you would report this to us. Please visit www.packtpub.com/support/errata and fill in the form.

Piracy: If you come across any illegal copies of our works in any form on the internet, we would be grateful if you would provide us with the location address or website name. Please contact us at copyright@packt.com with a link to the material.

If you are interested in becoming an author: If there is a topic that you have expertise in and you are interested in either writing or contributing to a book, please visit authors.packtpub.com.

Share Your Thoughts

Once you've read *Mastering SOLIDWORKS Sheet Metal*, we'd love to hear your thoughts! Scan the QR code below to go straight to the Amazon review page for this book and share your feedback.

https://packt.link/r/1803245247

Your review is important to us and the tech community and will help us make sure we're delivering excellent quality content.

Section 1: Getting Started with the Sheet Metal Module

Each journey starts with a first step. Our first goal will be to introduce what SolidWorks Sheet Metal is and how we can use it. We'll then explore the basics of creating and using simple Sheet Metal models and drawings.

This section contains the following chapters:

- *Chapter 1, Sheet Metal Basics – Exploring Sheet Metal Properties and Material Selection*

- *Chapter 2, Adding Bends Using Edge Flanges*

- *Chapter 3, Getting Familiar with Basic Tools in Sheet Metal*

- *Chapter 4, Creating Sheet Metal Drawings and Exporting Files*

1

Sheet Metal Basics – Exploring Sheet Metal Properties and Material Selection

SolidWorks is one of the world's premier **three-dimensional (3D) computer-aided design (CAD)** modeling software, with millions of users. However, while many people use SolidWorks for 3D solid modeling, there are also a number of more specialist modules for creating other types of models. The SolidWorks Sheet Metal module is one of the most important of these because it unlocks the massive potential of sheet metal manufacturing and production.

In this chapter, we'll explore what sheet metal is and why it is important. We'll learn how to create a Sheet Metal model using a **Base Flange** and how to edit the model's **Sheet Metal properties**.

We'll also cover **Flattening** *parts* and have a brief look at which materials are most commonly used for sheet metal.

By the end of this chapter, you'll understand how to start Sheet Metal *parts* and how to adjust their basic parameters, as well as having some wider knowledge of sheet metal manufacturing and use.

In this chapter, we're going to cover the following main topics:

- Introducing Sheet Metal

- Creating a **Base Flange**

- **Sheet Metal** properties

- Other **Base Flange** options and flattening parts

- Considerations when selecting sheet metal materials

Technical requirements

To complete this section and all following sections, you will require a copy of the SolidWorks software program, along with basic working knowledge. This includes how to carry out operations such as starting new *parts*, creating and editing sketches and features, and using common tools. For readers who are completely new to SolidWorks, it is advisable to gain a firm foundation of solid modeling first, before undertaking the Sheet Metal module covered in this book.

During the course of the book, if a certain tutorial or tool is causing problems, then try double-checking all of the previous steps, or even try closing the *part* and starting again from the beginning.

Error messages in SolidWorks can be quite descriptive and often tell the user exactly what the issue is. So, if presented with an error, then try to avoid the temptation to click **OK** without reading it properly, and attempt to carry out the action suggested in the message.

If the problems persist, then feel free to contact me online via Twitter at `www.twitter.com/johnoellison`.

SolidWorks versions

The examples and demonstrations in this book were made using SolidWorks 2021. Other versions of SolidWorks may have very minor differences in things such as the interface and how certain options are labeled, but in general, the workflow should be very similar. If you do get stuck on any of these differences, then please contact me using the details previously provided.

Units of measurement

Throughout this book, **millimeters (mm)** are used as the unit of measurement, but this can be adjusted according to the reader's preference by setting the model's units to **inches** ("), for example, and then typing the millimeter numerical value followed by mm into the **Smart Dimension** tool when adding dimensions. This will automatically convert the millimeter values into inches (or your selected unit type).

Terminology

Throughout this book, "sheet metal" (lowercase) refers to the general industry and manufacturing methods used in the real world, whereas "Sheet Metal" (capitalized) refers specifically to the SolidWorks Sheet Metal module.

The term "part" refers to a real-life component or item, whereas *part* (italicized) refers specifically to a SolidWorks *part* document.

Introducing Sheet Metal

Sheet metal parts are those that are—as the name suggests—created from flat sheets of metal. Numerous different manufacturing techniques such as bending, cutting, and forming allow these simple flat sheets to be transformed into complex 3D parts. The popularity of sheet metal has exploded in modern times because it allows designers and engineers to take a widely available material type—the flat sheets—and use relatively low-cost tools and processes to create complex products, at an industrial scale.

The chances are that a quick look around your home, garage, or workplace will reveal dozens of items that were created using sheet metal techniques. These can range from very simple items such as right-angle brackets to more complex products such as furniture, all the way up to detailed designs such as computer or electronics enclosures. Sheet metal is also used to create very complex items such as aircraft parts or car bodywork, although the most advanced formed parts are beyond the scope of SolidWorks Sheet Metal.

Figure 1.1: Examples of sheet metal parts

The beauty of the SolidWorks Sheet Metal module is that it allows users to create these 3D shapes, then flatten them down to sheets, and export them as **two-dimensional (2D)** designs that can be used for manufacturing.

Another great aspect of SolidWorks Sheet Metal is that, despite the name, it doesn't have to be used for purely metal parts. Sheet Metal can be used to create any kind of flattened 3D part, regardless of the real-life material. Try to think beyond the "metal" title, and a wide range of other uses can be unlocked. For example, Sheet Metal can be used to create cardboard packaging. This can be modeled in 3D before being virtually unfolded to be printed, cut out with a die-cutter, and then turned into 3D boxes. Sheet Metal can also even be used to create items as diverse as paper origami artwork.

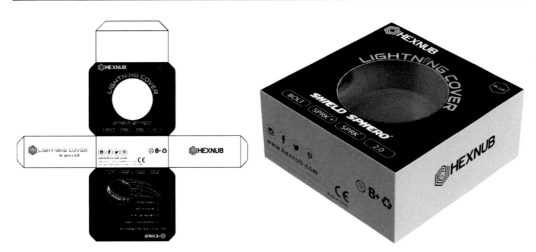

Figure 1.2: Sheet Metal isn't just for metal but any material, such as this cardboard packaging

Sheet Metal is a diverse set of manufacturing methods that will take your modeling and design to the next level. In summary:

- Sheet metal uses flat sheets to create 2D or 3D parts.
- Techniques include cutting, bending, and forming.
- SolidWorks Sheet Metal parts don't have to be metal!

In the next section, we'll look at how we can actually start making Sheet Metal *parts* in SolidWorks by creating a **Base Flange** that will be the foundation feature of these *parts*.

Creating a Base Flange

SolidWorks Sheet Metal *parts* can be started in two main ways—either by creating a **Base Flange** or by converting existing 3D *parts* into Sheet Metal *parts*. This section will cover the use of **Base Flanges**, which are the simplest but also the most flexible way to start new Sheet Metal *parts*.

Setting up the workspace

Before learning more about **Base Flanges**, let's first ensure that the workspace is set up correctly for Sheet Metal modeling. The Sheet Metal tools can be found via the **Insert** menu on the top menu bar (*Figure 1.3*) but it is faster and more convenient to use the **Sheet Metal** tab or toolbar:

Figure 1.3: The Sheet Metal tools in the Insert menu

Setting up the Sheet Metal tab or toolbar

To add the **Sheet Metal** tab, proceed as follows:

1. From within a SolidWorks *part* document, right-click on any of the existing tabs, or in any empty space, on the **Command Manager** (labeled **i** in *Figure 1.4*).

2. Select the **Tabs** sub-option (labeled **ii** in *Figure 1.4*) and ensure that there is a check mark next to the **Sheet Metal** option (labeled **iii** in *Figure 1.4*).

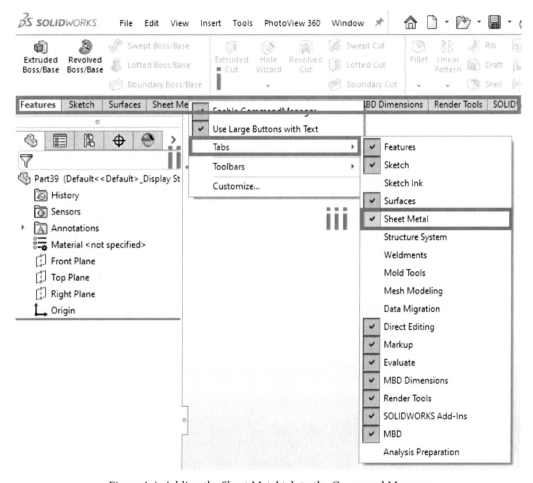

Figure 1.4: Adding the Sheet Metal tab to the Command Manager

This will then add the **Sheet Metal** tab to the existing tabs of the **Command Manager**.

To add the **Sheet Metal** toolbar:

1. The **Sheet Metal** toolbar can be added in a similar way to the tab. First, right-click on any of the existing tabs, or in an empty space, on the **Command Manager** (labeled **i** in *Figure 1.4*).

2. Select the **Toolbars** sub-option and ensure that there is a check mark next to the **Sheet Metal** option.

> **Should You Use the Sheet Metal Toolbar or the Sheet Metal Tab?**
>
> By default, the **Sheet Metal** tab and toolbar both contain the same set of tools. Either can be used throughout the book and this is a matter of user preference.
>
> The **Sheet Metal** tab contains larger, clearer icons, but the toolbar can be moved into the **Graphics Area** for easier access to tools.

Making a Base Flange

A **Base Flange** is the first feature of a Sheet Metal *part* and is the simplest way to create new Sheet Metal *parts*, while also offering the most flexibility. This is because once a **Base Flange** has been created, additional features such as bends and flanges can be added to build up a 3D *part* in a similar way to standard solid modeling. By contrast, converting existing *parts* to Sheet Metal (as covered later in the book) can limit the type of *part* that can be created and reduce editing options at later stages.

To actually create a **Base Flange**, a profile first needs to be sketched. Various profile types can be used, but this section will cover the simplest: a **Single Closed** profile.

To create a **Base Flange**:

1. Start a new SolidWorks *part*.

2. Start a sketch on the appropriate Plane, such as the **Top Plane** (labeled **i** in *Figure 1.5*).

3. Sketch the **Base Flange** profile. Different profile types will be covered later in the chapter, but for now, simply create a closed profile, such as a **Center Rectangle** (labeled **ii** in *Figure 1.5*).

4. Fully Define the profile by using the **Smart Dimension** tool and linking it to the **Origin** (labeled **iii** in *Figure 1.5*). Make the rectangle 200mm high and 300mm wide.

Fully Defining Sketches

During SolidWorks modeling, it is important to Fully Define sketches to ensure that the Sketch Entities are fixed and will not behave in unexpected ways, such as moving position. Fully Defined Sketch Entities will turn black, and when a sketch is Fully Defined, this will be indicated in the lower right of the screen (labeled **iv** in *Figure 1.5*).

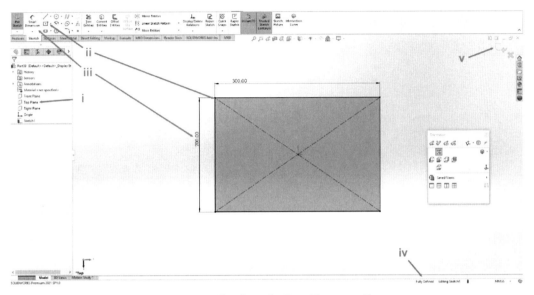

Figure 1.5: Sketching the Base Flange profile

5. Exit the sketch (labeled **v** in *Figure 1.5*).

6. Select the **Sheet Metal** tab or toolbar and select the **Base Flange/Tab** option—this should be the first icon (labeled **i** in *Figure 1.6*).

7. You will be prompted to select a sketch. Select the previous sketch that was just drawn and a yellow preview of the **Base Flange** should appear (see *Figure 1.6*).

Note

It is also possible to skip *Step 5* and select the **Base Flange/Tab** option directly from within the sketch. In this case, the sketch that is being edited will automatically be used.

8. Enter the following settings (these will be covered in more detail later in the chapter):

- **Thickness**: 1mm

- **Bend Allowance**: K-Factor, 0.5

- **Auto Relief**: Rectangular

- **Ratio**:0.5 (labeled **iii** in *Figure 1.6*)

    Press **OK** (labeled **iv** in Figure 1.6) and the **Base Flange** feature is created.

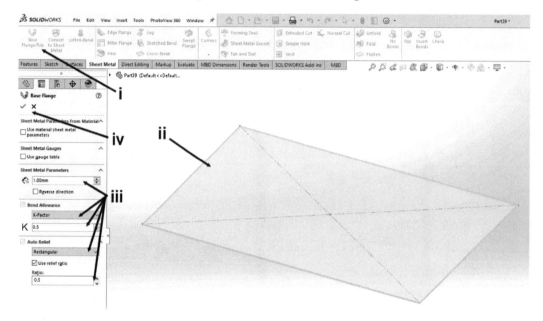

Figure 1.6: Creating a Base Flange feature

The **Base Flange** feature is now created, and Base-Flange1 (note: your number may differ) appears in the FeatureManager Design Tree at the left of the screen (labeled **i** in *Figure 1.7*). This feature can be edited and adjusted in the usual way by left-clicking on the feature and selecting **Edit Feature**.

Creating a **Base Flange** feature turns the entire *part* into a Sheet Metal *part* and so automatically adds some extra items to the FeatureManager Design Tree. These items indicate that a *part* is a Sheet Metal model, and they are made up of the following:

- Sheet-Metal folder: This contains all of the global properties of your Sheet Metal *part*, such as the **Thickness** and the **Bend Radius** properties (labeled **ii** in *Figure 1.7*).

- `Flat-Pattern` folder: This folder contains a flattened version of the *part* (labeled **iii** in *Figure 1.7*). By default, this folder will be suppressed, so it will appear grayed out at this stage, but this will be covered in more detail later in the chapter.

- `Cut list` folder: This folder contains all of the separate sheets that make up the *part*. It can be thought of in a similar way to the `Solid Bodies` folder that is used in normal solid modeling

  The number in brackets after the folder name indicates how many sheets make up the *part*. For example, a *part* with two separate body and lid sheets would show `(2)` after the `Cut list` folder (labeled **iv** in *Figure 1.7*).

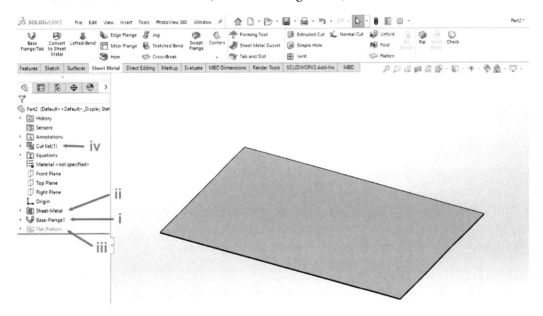

Figure 1.7: Sheet Metal part details

Base Flanges are usually the best way of starting your Sheet Metal *parts* and are often the first feature created in a Sheet Metal *part*. They can be made by sketching a closed profile, then selecting the **Base Flange/Tab** option from the Sheet Metal tools.

Adding a **Base Flange** feature will turn the *part* into a Sheet Metal *part* and will automatically add the `Flat-Pattern`, `Cut list`, and `Sheet-Metal` folders, which we will explore more in the following section.

> **Saving Parts**
>
> At this stage, your current *part* can be saved as we will continue using this document throughout the book.
>
> When working in SolidWorks, try to get into the habit of regularly saving your work, as a safeguard against crashes and other problems.

Sheet Metal properties

Sheet Metal properties are global settings that apply to the entire *part*. This section shows how to adjust these properties and what they actually mean. The section contains some background theory that is fairly dry but is an important foundation for understanding Sheet Metal. Some of this underlying theory will become much clearer once we actually start to use and demonstrate the tools later in the book, so don't worry too much if certain parts of it still appear a little confusing at this stage.

There are four Sheet Metal properties:

1. **Sheet Thickness**
2. **Bend Radius**
3. **Bend Allowance**
4. **Auto Relief**

Editing the Sheet Metal properties and adjusting the Sheet Thickness

As previously mentioned, Sheet Metal *parts* are usually made from sheets with a constant thickness. Therefore, the **thickness** of a *part* is an important aspect of Sheet Metal.

To edit the **Sheet Metal** properties of a *part*, simply left- or right-click on the Sheet-Metal folder in the FeatureManager Design Tree (labeled **ii** in *Figure 1.7*) and select **Edit Feature**.

To set the thickness, adjust the value under the **Thickness** field (labeled **i** in *Figure 1.8*) and press the green **OK** check mark. For example, try setting 2mm thickness and pressing **OK**. You should now see that the thickness of the **Base Flange** has changed from 1mm to 2mm.

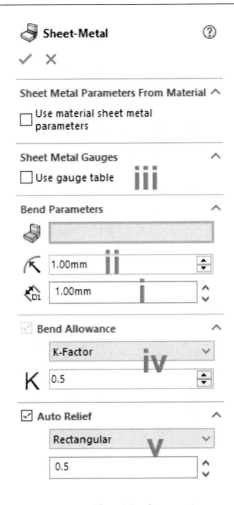

Figure 1.8: Sheet Metal properties

This **Thickness** setting is global throughout the entire *part*, so any new features that are added, such as **Edge Flanges**, will also be made using this same thickness. Editing one single value in the `Sheet-Metal` folder provides a very simple way to adjust the entire *part* and all of the features that make it up.

Editing the Bend Radius

Along with the thickness, another very important property of Sheet Metal *parts* is the **Bend Radius**.

Whenever a flat sheet of metal is bent or folded to create 3D parts, the corners that are created by the bending process will never be completely square. Even with a very thin and flexible material, such as aluminium foil, a small bend radius is needed.

This is also true in SolidWorks Sheet Metal: *a bend radius is always required* (*Figure 1.9*), even if it is tiny.

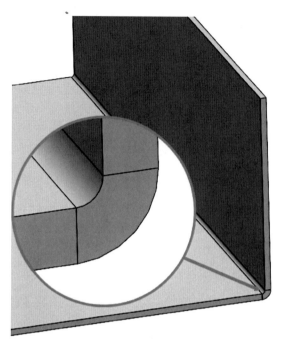

Figure 1.9: A bend radius is always needed

In SolidWorks Sheet Metal the **Bend Radius** refers to the size of the inside of bends, and it can be set in the **Sheet Metal** properties.

Simply edit the **Sheet Metal** properties and adjust the value (labeled **ii** in *Figure 1.8*).

By default, the **Bend Radius** that is set in the **Sheet Metal** properties will apply to any features that are added to the *part*, although the **Bend Radius** can be overridden for specific bends, and this will be covered later in the book.

What size should we set the Bend Radius to?

Although setting the **Bend Radius** value itself is straightforward, how do we actually know what value to use for it? **Bend Radius** depends on a number of factors, such as the material type, the manufacturing method, and the thickness of the material. In general, as the sheet thickness increases, the bend radius value also increases. To visualize this, think about bending a very thin sheet of metal foil, compared to bending a thick plate—the thinner sheet will allow a much tighter bend to be created.

General figures for steel bending might be something like this:

Sheet Thickness	Bend Radius
1mm	R1.4mm
2mm	R1.88mm
3mm	R2.75mm
4mm	R3.0mm
5mm	R3.6mm

There are a number of ways to determine the **Bend Radius**.

- **Speak to your manufacturer**. The most reliable method of determining the **Bend Radius** is usually to talk directly to the people making your *parts*. Tell them what you're planning to create, and the material type and thickness, and they should be able to recommend certain settings to use.

- **Search online or in reference books**. Try searching for a phrase such as `1mm thick steel bending radius`. The results should give you a good idea of suitable values to start your design, which can then be fine-tuned at a later stage by adjusting the Sheet Metal properties.

- **Use the SolidWorks Gauge Tables**. Gauge numbers are a way of measuring the thickness of metal sheets based on weight. SolidWorks contains gauge tables that are a list of preset sizes that are built into SolidWorks Sheet Metal. They can be used to find common **Bend Radius** values.

To activate the **Gauge Tables**:

I.   Put a check in the **Use gauge table** box at the top of the **Sheet Metal** properties (labeled **iii** in *Figure 1.8*). A table can then be selected from the drop-down list.

> **Note**
> SolidWorks Gauge Tables require Microsoft Excel to be installed on the computer and will not work without it.

II. Try selecting a table such as the `SAMPLE TABLE – STEEL` (*Figure 1.10*). The thickness of the Sheet Metal *part* can now be set using the gauge numbers from the dropdown list, rather than the specific thickness value.

III. Experiment with different sizes to see how the gauge number relates to actual thickness:

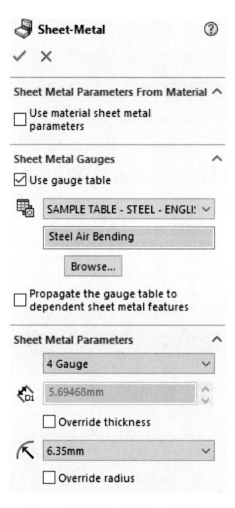

Figure 1.10: Using the Gauge Tables

> **Note**
>
> A higher gauge number corresponds to a thinner sheet. It can be seen in *Figure 1.10* that **4 Gauge** steel is 5.69mm thick, whereas **16 Gauge** steel is only 1.51mm thick.

As the gauge number is changed, you'll notice that the **Bend Radius** value also automatically changes to correspond to the new sheet sizes. As expected, thicker sheets require a higher **Bend Radius** value.

Exercise Caution When Using Gauge Numbers!

Gauge numbers are specific to the material used, so confusion is easily caused. For example, a given gauge number of steel is **not the same thickness** as one in aluminum. **16 Gauge** steel is 1.52mm thick, but **16 Gauge** aluminum is only 1.29mm thick. For this reason, many international standards organizations recommend against the use of gauge numbers and instead suggest specifying the sheet thickness using dimensions.

The Gauge Tables can give a good indication of bend radii, but I recommend using them as a guide only, and instead directly setting and specifying sheet thicknesses.

The **Bend Radius** is a vital *aspect* of SolidWorks Sheet Metal and is needed for every bent *part*. It can be set in the **Sheet Metal** properties as a global value, but can also be overridden for certain bends if needed.

Get an idea of the **Bend Radius** needed by either speaking to your manufacturer, searching online, or using **Gauge Tables**. However, if using gauge numbers and tables, be careful to ensure your material choice is correct and clearly marked on any drawings. It is wise to use gauge tables as a guide only, and instead (or in addition to this) specify an exact sheet thickness.

Understanding the Bend Allowance

The next Sheet Metal property that affects your models is the **Bend Allowance** property (labeled **iv** in *Figure 1.8*). This allows us to accurately calculate the size of bent *parts* once they have been unfolded into a flat sheet.

To understand what exactly the **Bend Allowance** property is and why it is important, let's look at a simple *part* from the side. This consists of a **Base Flange** and one single **Edge Flange**, as illustrated in *Figure 1.11*.

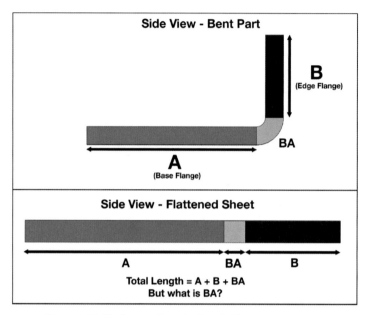

Figure 1.11: Understanding the Bend Allowance property

We can see that the size of the Sheet Metal *part* will be the length of the **Base Flange** (**A** in *Figure 1.11*) plus the length of the **Edge Flange** (**B** in *Figure 1.11*), plus the size of the area of the bend itself (**BA** or **Bend Allowance** in *Figure 1.11*). Therefore, when the *part* is flattened, the total size of the sheet that we require will be **A + B + BA**.

However, depending on how and where the bend length (**BA**) is measured, we may end up with different values. For example, if the inside of the bend is measured, the length may be 5mm, but if the outside of the bend is measured then the length will be longer— 15mm in this case, as illustrated in *Figure 1.12*.

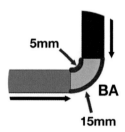

Figure 1.12: The size of the bend depends on where exactly is measured

The length of **BA** is determined by the **Bend Allowance** in the **Sheet Metal** properties, and there are a number of different options to set the **Bend Allowance**.

These **Bend Allowance** options are:

- **Bend Table**
- **K-Factor**
- **Bend Allowance**
- **Bend Deduction**
- **Bend Calculation**

Each option will give slightly different end results, but if you're unsure which option to use, then it's usually best to use the **K-Factor** bend allowance.

What Is the K-Factor Bend Allowance?

K-Factor is a way of working out the size needed for bends in sheet metal. Whenever a metal sheet is bent, there will always be a region of the bend, inside the bend, where the material is compressed, and another region, outside of the bend, where the material is stretched. At a certain point within a cross-section of the sheet, there will be a boundary where the compression and stretching exactly cancel each other out. Along this boundary, there will be no change of length in the material. The K-Factor is the name given to a line along this boundary, where no change in length occurs between flat and folded *parts* (*Figure 1.13*).

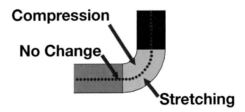

Figure 1.13: The K-Factor is an imaginary line through a cross-section of the material, where there is no change in size between the bent part and the flat part

The K-Factor is a ratio, so it will always be between 0 and 1. The inside of the bend is a K-Factor of 0 and the outside of the bend is a K-Factor of 1. Therefore, the middle of the bend is a K-Factor of 0.5, as illustrated in *Figure 1.14*.

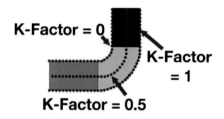

Figure 1.14: The K-Factor is a ratio indicating a line through a cross-section of the bend

What Value of K-Factor Should I Use?

The K-Factor depends on a number of factors, such as material and bending type. If you're unsure about what to use, then a K-Factor of 0.5 is usually a good estimate for most parts and materials.

You can also try asking your manufacturer what value they recommend you should use.

The K-Factor is the easiest way to work out **Bend Allowances** and can easily be changed at a later stage if needed, by editing the **Sheet Metal** properties.

Other Bend Allowance options

As well as the K-Factor, there are also some other ways of calculating the **Bend Allowance**. If you are unfamiliar with these methods, then it is highly recommended that you use the **K-Factor** option, as detailed previously. The other **Bend Allowance** options are:

- **Bend Allowance**: This allows you to specifically define the length of the **Bend Allowance**. This can be useful if a manufacturer gives you a certain value to use. However, this option should be used with care as any value can be inputted. Therefore, if an incorrect value is used, this can result in completely wrong sizes on **Flat Pattern** *parts*.

- **Bend Deduction**: This option is somewhat similar to the **Bend Allowance** option but it measures the outside length of the folded *part*, then removes (or deducts) a certain value. Again, if you are unfamiliar with this method, use it cautiously, as using the wrong **Bend Deduction** value can give unusable results.

- **Bend Table**: This option allows a Bend Table to be created in Microsoft Excel. This table can specify Bend Allowance or Deduction values based on exact bend details, such as the radius and angle.

- **Bend Calculation**: Finally, the **Bend Calculation** option allows the use of equations to calculate the bending allowance based on factors such as the material's thickness, K-Factor, and the bend radius.

The **Bend Allowance** option is an important factor in ensuring that you are able to use the correct size of flat sheet to make your final, bent parts. A number of options are available, but if you're unfamiliar with **Bend Allowance**, then it is recommended that you simply use the **K-Factor** option. A **K-Factor** value of 0.5 gives a good estimation for most parts, and your manufacturer should be able to advise you in more detail, based on the material type and your exact part details.

Auto Relief options

The final Sheet Metal property is **Auto Relief**. This is a way of automatically adding relief cuts to bends if they are required. *Figure 1.15* shows a simple **Base Flange** with an **Edge Flange** that only runs part of the way along the edge. In order to create this specific type of bend, **Auto Relief** cuts are needed; otherwise, the metal won't be able to bend correctly:

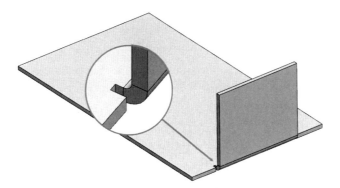

Figure 1.15: An example of an Auto Relief cut

Auto Relief cuts aren't needed on all bend types and will be automatically added when they are required. However, the exact type of relief cut is what is specified in the **Auto Relief** option.

The three types are:

- **Rectangular**: This gives a rectangular cut (see *Figure 1.16*). The size of the cut is determined by the ratio number and is related to the thickness of the sheet—for example, a ratio of `0.5` and a sheet thickness of `1`mm will give a relief cut 0.5mm wide, which extends 0.5mm beyond the bend region. Note: the relief ratio has to be between 0.05 and 2.0.

- **Obround**: This gives a more rounded cut (see *Figure 1.16*) and also uses a ratio based on the thickness of the sheet in the same way as the **Rectangular** option.

- **Tear**: This option essentially tears the metal, without providing a visible cut area. This is the minimum that is needed to be able to flatten and bend the *part*.

All three options are depicted here:

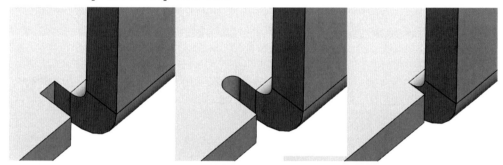

Figure 1.16: Auto Relief examples; left to right: Rectangular, Obround, Tear

Auto Relief cuts are an important requirement for some bend types but they will be added automatically, so this option can usually be set to **Rectangular** or **Obround** with a ratio of 0.5 unless you have specific requirements.

A recap of Sheet Metal properties

Sheet Metal properties are an important way of defining your Sheet Metal *part*. They can be adjusted by editing the `Sheet-Metal` folder within the FeatureManager Design Tree. They generally apply to the whole *part*, although they can often be overridden for specific features.

The four options are:

- **Thickness**: This determines the thickness of the sheet used to create the **Base Flange** and subsequent features.

- **Bend Radius**: This sets the internal size of bends. A **Bend Radius** is always required for bent edges in SolidWorks Sheet Metal.

- **Bend Allowance**: This allows us to accurately calculate the correct size of flat sheet that can be used to create bent *parts*. There are a number of ways to calculate the **Bend Allowance**, but if you are unsure, then the best option is usually a **K-Factor** value of 0.5.

- **Auto Relief**: Some bends require relief cuts in order for them to be flattened or folded correctly. These will be added automatically if needed, but this option controls the size and type of cut.

Now that we have learned the basics of Sheet Metal properties and creating **Base Flanges**, we can go on to explore how 3D *parts* can be flattened, as well as more advanced types of **Base Flanges**.

Other Base Flange options and flattening parts

In the previous section, we introduced **Base Flanges**, which are usually the first feature of your Sheet Metal *part*. As an example, we sketched a simple rectangle and then used this to make a rectangular **Base Flange**. This type of **Base Flange** is called a **Single Closed** profile because it only contains one single profile and that profile is closed (that is, it has no open areas or gaps in the outer perimeter). This can be seen in *Figure 1.17*.

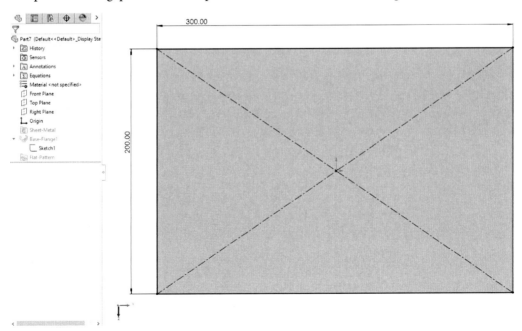

Figure 1.17: A Single Closed profile contains one single profile, which is closed

However, two other options can be useful for creating different kinds of **Base Flanges**. These are the **Multiple Contained Closed** and the **Single Open Contour** profiles. It's not too important to remember the specific names, as long as you know how to use each type.

Multiple Contained Closed

For our previous **Base Flange**, we just used one single closed profile, but closed profiles can also contain *other closed profiles* within them. This type is known as **Multiple Contained Closed** and can be useful for adding holes and cutouts to your **Base Flange**. An example of this is shown in *Figure 1.18*.

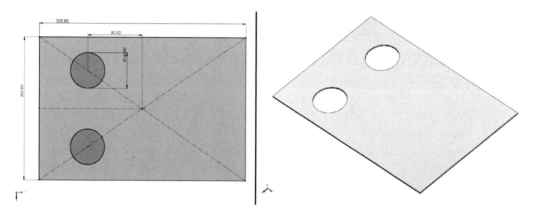

Figure 1.18: Multiple Contained Closed Base Flanges can contain smaller closed profiles within one larger closed profile

Although using the **Multiple Contained Closed** option for creating **Base Flanges** can sometimes save time, I would personally recommend creating very simple **Base Flanges** and then adding extra cutouts and holes as separate features. This approach just makes it easier to adjust or remove extra details later on, if needed.

Single Open Contour

Instead of using closed profiles, it is also possible to create **Base Flanges** using open profiles known as **Single Open Contours**. These can range from a simple, single line, up to more complex collections of Sketch Entities.

To create a basic **Single Closed Contour Base Flange**:

1. Start a new *part* document and start a sketch on the appropriate Plane, such as the **Front Plane**.

2. Sketch the **Base Flange**. It can be easiest to think of the **Single Open Contour** option as a side view or cross-section view of the flange. For the first example, try a single horizontal line, 100mm long, using the **Line** tool (see *Figure 1.19*).

3. Remember to Fully Define your sketch by starting from the Origin and using the **Smart Dimension** tool to set the line's length.

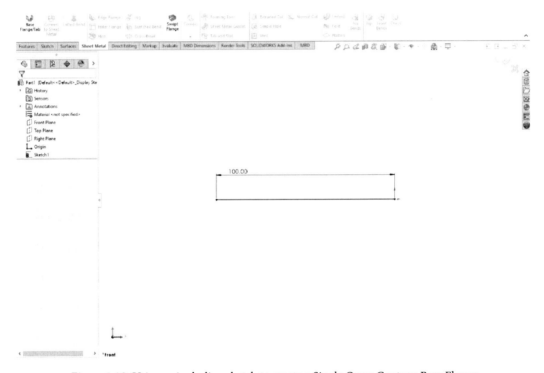

Figure 1.19: Using a single-line sketch to create a Single Open Contour Base Flange

4. Select the **Base Flange/Tab** option from the **Sheet Metal** tab or toolbar.

5. The width of the **Base Flange** can be set using the **Direction 1** (and **Direction 2**, if required) options in the **Property Manager** on the left of the screen. The **Sheet Metal** properties can also be set at this stage (see *Figure 1.20*).

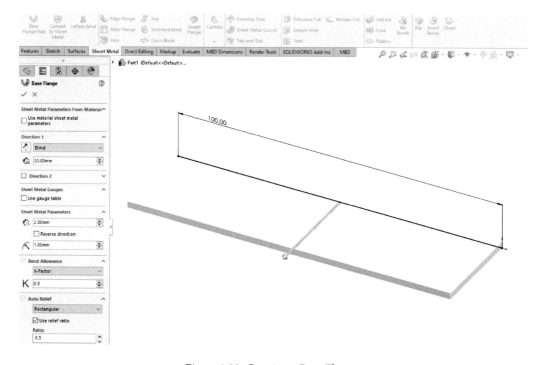

Figure 1.20: Creating a Base Flange

6. Press **OK** to create a **Base Flange**. It can be seen that this creates a simple, rectangular **Base Flange** similar to the **Single Closed Profile** example from the first section.

In this way, the **Single Open Contour Base Flange** can be thought of as similar to the **Thin Feature Extrude** option from normal solid modeling.

Creating more Base Flange complex shapes

The real beauty of using the **Single Open Contour** option is that it allows you to easily create more complex, bent shapes in one feature.

1. Start a new part document and start a sketch on the appropriate Plane, such as the **Front Plane**.

2. Sketch a more complex shape using the **Line** tool. An example *Z* or jog shape can be seen in *Figure 1.21*.

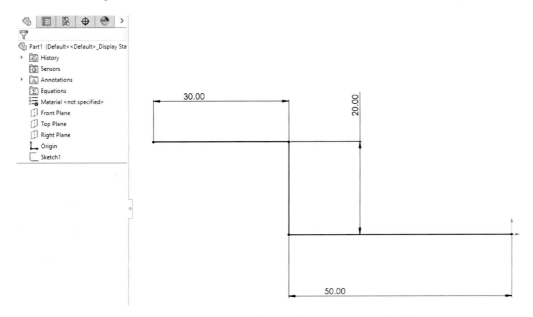

Figure 1.21: A more complex Single Open Contour sketch

3. Select **Base Flange/Tab** from the **Sheet Metal** tools and set your desired options. Example settings could be:

  - **Width**: 10mm, Direction 1

  - **Thickness**: 2mm

  - **Bend Radius**: 1mm

4.   Press **OK** to create a **Base Flange** (*Figure 1.22*). It can be seen that although the underlying sketch had sharp corners, the actual **Base Flange** feature has automatically been created with the bent corners using the **Bend Radius** that was specified in the **Sheet Metal** properties:

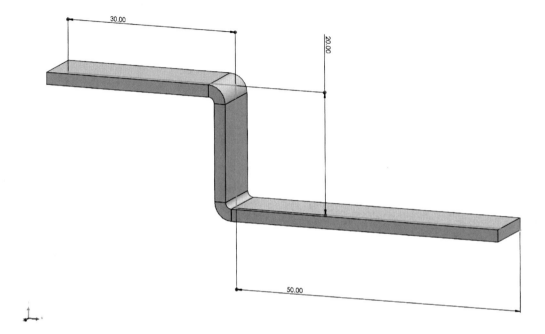

Figure 1.22: Single Open Contour Base Flange

Using Single Open Contours to create **Base Flanges** can be a good way to simplify the production of parts such as simple brackets.

Note that these types of sketches don't just need to use straight lines—they can also use arcs and splines if required.

Flattening parts

Now that we have created a *part* with bends in it, we can explore how 3D Sheet Metal *parts* can be flattened. Flattening is one of the features of the SolidWorks Sheet Metal module that really does add huge value to the design process because it allows *parts* to be accurately converted from finished *parts* into a state that can be easily created from sheets of flat stock material.

To flatten Sheet Metal *parts*:

1. From within a Sheet Metal *part*, select the **Flatten** option from the **Sheet Metal** tab or toolbar (labeled **i** in *Figure 1.23*).

2. The *part* will be unfolded into a flat sheet. Note the dotted outline, which indicates the bounding box of the flattened *part*, and the sketch lines, which show the location of Bend Lines (labeled **ii** in *Figure 1.23*).

3. If your Bend Lines aren't visible, try going to **View | Hide/Show | Sketches**.

4. Note also that the Flat-Pattern folder at the end of the FeatureManager Design Tree is now unsuppressed and so is no longer grayed out (labeled **iii** in *Figure 1.23*).

   Using the **Flatten** option essentially unsuppresses (or switches on) the Flat-Pattern folder, which flattens the *part*. If you expand the Flat-Pattern folder, then the **Flat Pattern** feature will be seen, and this contains the bend details of the *part*.

5. To unflatten—or fold up—the *part*, simply click the **Flatten** button on the **Sheet Metal** tab or toolbar again or click the **Flatten** button that can be seen in the top right of the graphics area (labeled **iv** in *Figure 1.23*). Note that the *part* folds up and the Flat-Pattern folder is now suppressed (or switched off) again.

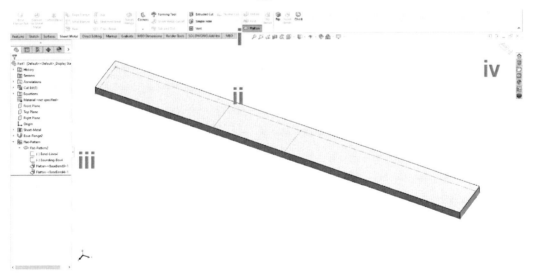

Figure 1.23: Flatten option

The **Flatten** option is a vital aspect of SolidWorks Sheet Metal that allows *parts* to be unfolded. As we progress through the book and learn about the Sheet Metal tools, we will see this option in use in a more practical setting.

A recap of Base Flange options and flattening parts

There are three types of **Base Flange** (See *Fig. 1.24*):

1. **Single Closed Profile**: This is one of the most basic types of **Base Flange** and uses one single profile that is fully closed, such as a simple rectangle or square. Although it is simple, this type of **Base Flange** is extremely useful and is likely to make up the majority of **Base Flanges** for Sheet Metal *parts*.

2. **Multiple Contained Closed**: Closed profiles can also contain smaller, closed profiles such as cutouts and holes. While these types of **Base Flanges** can be useful in certain situations, it is generally better practice to create simple **Base Flanges** using a **Single Closed Profile** and then add any extra holes, cuts, or details as separate features. This makes modification of these features at a later stage much easier.

3. **Single Open Contour**: **Base Flanges** can also be created using a collection of single Sketch Entities such as lines, arcs, and splines. This type of **Base Flange** can be useful when creating items such as brackets.

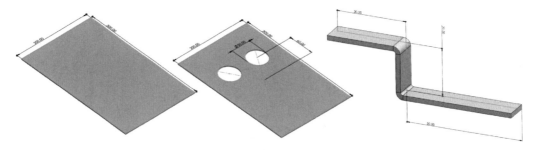

Figure 1.24: Types of Base Flange; left to right: Single Closed Profile, Multiple Contained Closed, Single Open Contour

Flattening is a vital aspect of SolidWorks Sheet Metal and *parts* with bends can be flattened by simply selecting the **Flatten** option from the Sheet Metal tools. This will unsuppress the Flat-Pattern folder and unfold any bends in the *part*.

So far in this chapter, we have learned how to start Sheet Metal *parts* and how to create the first feature of most of these *parts*—the **Base Flange**. We have also looked at how to edit the various Sheet Metal properties that are important to those *parts*. So, now that we have a reasonable idea of how to start *virtual* Sheet Metal *parts*, we will jump briefly into a real-world aspect of sheet metal and take a look at the various sheet metal materials available.

Considerations when selecting sheet metal materials

There are dozens of types of metal that could be used to create sheet metal parts and these all vary in use, physical properties, cost, and availability. The following pages will give you an idea of which might be best for your project.

This section is not an exhaustive list of materials; rather, it is just an overview of some of the most common ones that you are likely to encounter. Within these materials, there are also many specific grades (sub-types) of metal, each with slightly different properties. If in doubt, discuss your needs and budget with your sheet metal manufacturer and your material supplier to find the most suitable choice for your needs.

Steel and aluminum

The vast majority of sheet metal parts around us are made from either steel or aluminum, and of those, steel is probably the most common material.

Advantages and disadvantages of steel

Steel is an excellent all-round material, and if you're unsure which material to use, then steel is usually a solid choice. Steel is so popular and widely used for a number of reasons. It is very strong, easy to weld, and ductile, which means it is easy to bend and form compared to more exotic metals. Steel is also fairly inexpensive—it can be up to three times cheaper than aluminum for the same weight—and is widely available.

Material choice is always about compromise, so every material will have disadvantages. One of the main downsides of steel is that it is quite heavy—around two and a half times denser than aluminum, depending on the exact grades used. This means that if you have two pieces that are the exact same size and shape, then the steel part will be significantly heavier than the aluminum part.

Steel also has poor corrosion protection, meaning that it often goes rusty. You will have seen rusty steel items such as car bodywork. This rust is corrosion that is caused by a reaction between the metal and elements in the environment such as water and oxygen. The rust weakens and eventually destroys the metal. Steel can be treated to prevent or slow corrosion, but this will add to the material cost, and some other metals have much more natural resistance to corrosion.

Pros and cons of aluminum

Aluminum is the second-most common material used in sheet metal and is used in a wide range of items including bike frames, aircraft parts, and drinking cans.

One of the reasons why aluminum is so popular in the aerospace industry is that it is much lighter than steel. It also has excellent natural resistance to corrosion and so doesn't need extra surface treatments to stop it from going rusty. Another great property of aluminum is how malleable it is, meaning that it is very easy to bend. Consider how flexible aluminum foil is, or how easy it is to crush a drinks can.

Unfortunately, these positive properties also come with downsides, and aluminum is a lot more expensive than steel. However, because it is less dense, parts can be made lighter, which somewhat offsets this cost. Another factor is that although aluminum is lighter than steel, it is also weaker, meaning that parts that bear the same load will have to be made thicker in aluminum. However, due to the lower density of aluminum, these can actually be lighter than the equivalent steel parts. So overall, depending on exactly which grades of metal are used, aluminum generally has a better **strength-to-weight ratio** (**SWR**) than steel.

Other common metals

Steel and aluminum make up the vast majority of sheet metal parts but some other materials are reasonably common, such as the following:

- **Copper**: Copper is often used for parts such as electronics or heat-exchanging components because it has good electrical and thermal conductivity.

  It is also easy to bend and form and has good corrosion resistance, and so is often used in plumbing, to make pipes and fixtures. Copper is more expensive than steel and aluminum, and some areas have issues with copper theft due to the higher price of the metal.

- **Brass**: This metal is an alloy (a mixture) of copper and zinc that looks similar to copper but has a brighter, shinier look. For this reason, it is often used for decorative items such as door knockers, fixtures, and trinkets.

  It is extremely malleable and so is commonly used to make musical instruments in the brass section, such as trumpets. Brass has exceptional corrosion resistance and so is often seen in extreme environments, like door handles on ships. As with copper, it is quite an expensive metal and so is usually used sparingly.

- **Stainless steel**: Steel can be alloyed with other metals such as chromium to create different grades of stainless steel. This is steel that has a much greater resistance to corrosion than standard steel, while still retaining much of the strength and other benefits. For this reason, it is often used to make cutlery or surgical instruments.

  Stainless steel sheet metal parts include things like large items of kitchen equipment—for example, sinks and countertops. However, this improved corrosion resistance makes stainless steel much more expensive than standard steel.

This overview is not intended to be a complete list of metals, and other niche materials might include tin, gold, and titanium. Each of these will have specific properties that suit different applications and budgets. As mentioned earlier, it is wise to discuss your specific needs with your sheet metal supplier and manufacturer to get the best fit for your project.

A summary of sheet metal material properties can be seen in the following table:

Material Type	Advantages	Disadvantages
Steel	Strong, cheap, widely available; easy to work and weld	Heavy; poor corrosion resistance
Aluminum	Lightweight; good SWR; good corrosion resistance; malleable	More expensive than steel; lower strength than steel
Copper	Good thermal and electrical conductivity; good corrosion resistance; malleable	Expensive
Brass	Very malleable; good corrosion resistance	Expensive
Stainless steel	Similar benefits to steel but with excellent corrosion resistance	Expensive

Sheet metal thicknesses and sheet sizes

Depending on where you live in the world, sheet metal is usually sold either by gauge number or the actual thickness of the sheet. As previously mentioned, gauge numbers are a way of measuring sheet metal thickness based on the weight of the material, and generally, a higher gauge number means a thinner sheet.

Gauge numbers are specific for each material, so **16 gauge** steel will be a different thickness than **16 gauge** aluminum. Therefore, it is highly recommended that sheet thickness is also specified in actual thickness, to avoid any confusion.

Metal sheets are also available in a wide range of sheet sizes, both metric and imperial. Some common sizes are shown in *Figure 1.26* and include 48x120 " or 2x1 meters (m):

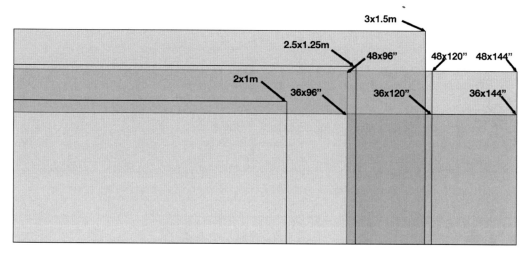

Figure 1.25: Common metal sheet sizes

When creating very big parts, or even large numbers of small parts, it is worth checking which sheet sizes are available to you and designing with this in mind. If making lots of small parts, it is even possible to use third-party "nesting" software to arrange the parts on the sheet in the most efficient way and avoid wasted material.

Material selection recap

Even when designing parts virtually in SolidWorks, it is important to consider how those parts will be created in the real world, and a vital aspect of this is the material choice. Most sheet metal parts are made from steel or aluminum, but other common metals include copper, brass, and stainless steel, and each of these materials has unique properties that suit different needs.

Sheet thicknesses are generally defined by actual thickness or using a gauge number. This is based on the material's weight, meaning that the same gauge number gives different thicknesses for different materials. Sheets come in a variety of common sizes that may have an impact on the design of your parts.

Summary

In this chapter, we introduced SolidWorks Sheet Metal and learned how to set up a Sheet Metal workspace and create **Base Flanges**. These are usually the first feature in a Sheet Metal *part*, and we covered the three different types: **Single Closed Profile**, **Multiple Contained Closed**, and **Single Open Contour**.

Next, we explored the four **Sheet Metal** properties—**Thickness**, **Bend Radius**, **Bend Allowance**, and **Auto Relief**—and how these can be edited to adjust the properties of the entire *part*.

Finally, we learned how 3D *parts* can be flattened, which is essential if they are to be made from metal sheets in the real world. On a similar note, we looked at common sheet metal materials and sheet sizes, and how these might be relevant to your final design.

In *Chapter 2, Adding Bends Using Edge Flanges*, we will start to build up a 3D design by learning how to use **Edge Flanges** to add extra detail to the **Base Flange**.

2
Adding Bends Using Edge Flanges

Bent edges known as **Edge Flanges** are the workhorses of **SolidWorks Sheet Metal**, and they are one of the most common building blocks for adding 3D detail to your flat **Base Flanges**. Although Edge Flanges can appear to be very simple, they can be used to build highly complex parts.

In this chapter, we'll learn how to add basic Edge Flanges, and then we'll explore how these can be edited and adjusted. We'll also look at some more advanced options and details that can unlock the power of Edge Flanges, allowing you to use them on multiple edges, as well as edit flange profiles, and more.

By the end of this chapter, you'll have a full understanding of Edge Flanges and how they can be used to build Sheet Metal models.

In this chapter, we're going to cover the following main topics:

- Using Edge Flanges
- Edge Flanges: advanced options

Using Edge Flanges

One of the most basic and common features in SolidWorks Sheet Metal is the Edge Flange. At its simplest, an Edge Flange is just a bent section of a metal sheet on an edge. A very simple sheet metal box consists of one single Base Flange with four Edge Flanges attached to it (one on each side as shown in *Figure 2.1*).

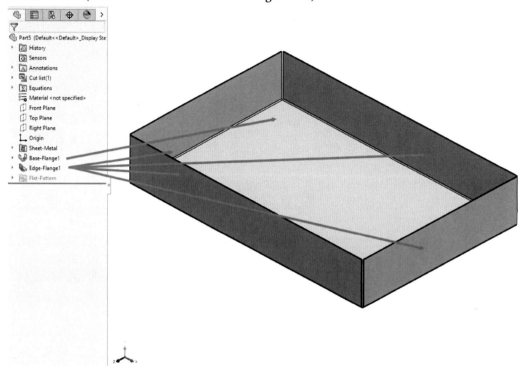

Figure 2.1: A simple box made from one Base Flange and four Edge Flanges

Individual Edge Flanges are extremely simple features but when combined, they can be used to create parts that are much more complex.

Creating your first Edge Flange

Edge Flanges are relatively simple to make:

1. Open your **Base Flange** *part from Chapter 1, Sheet Metal Basics – Exploring Sheet Metal Properties and Material Selection,* or create a new SolidWorks *part* and make a Base Flange that is 200 x 300 mm in size (as shown in *Chapter 1, Sheet Metal Basics – Exploring Sheet Metal Properties and Material Selection*).

2. The material Thickness should be 1 mm, with a Bend Radius of 1 mm (*Figure 2.2*).

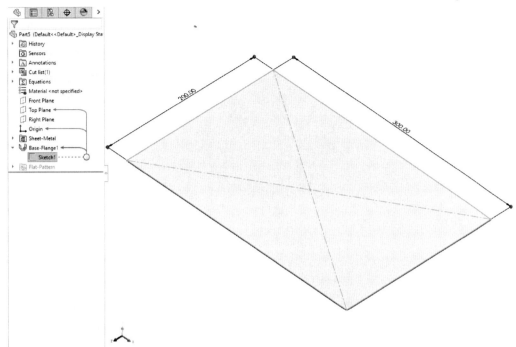

Figure 2.2: Creating a 200 x 300 mm Base Flange

3. To start adding Edge Flanges, select the **Edge Flange** option from the Sheet Metal tools (*Figure 2.3*).

Figure 2.3: The Edge Flange tool

4. Selecting the **Edge Flange** tool will open the **Edge Flange** Property Manager (*Figure 2.4*) and show a number of options. Although they look fairly complicated, not all of them are needed for every flange, and we will cover them step-by-step throughout this chapter.

The most important options are the **Flange Parameters**, **Angle**, and **Flange Length**

Figure 2.4: The Edge Flange Property Manager

5. **Edge selection**: Before we actually add any flanges, we first need to decide where we actually want to position them. To select the edges for the Edge Flanges, complete the following steps:

   I.   Ensure that you have selected the **Edge** selection box (*Figure 2.4*, (*i*)). This will be blue in color when selected.

   II.   Left-click on the edges in the model to select them. You may need to zoom in to select the edges you want.

   III. Try selecting one of the short edges by left-clicking it. You should see a yellow preview of the Edge Flange, which follows the mouse (*Figure 2.5*). This can be dragged out to the desired position, then a single left-click will set the length (see *Step 7* for more details on Flange Length).

IV.   Edges can be removed from the current selection by left-clicking them again or by right-clicking in the Edge selection box and choosing **Clear Selections** or **Delete**.

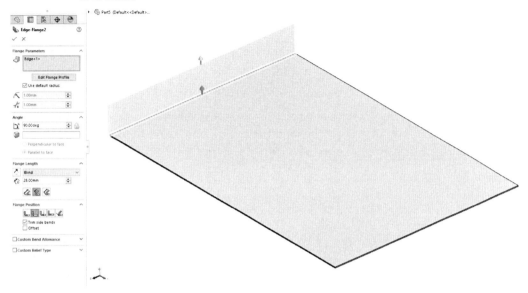

Figure 2.5: An Edge Flange preview

6.   **Bend Radius**: Note that the Bend Radius of the new Edge Flange appears near the top of the Property Manager (*Figure 2.4*, (*ii*)). This Bend Radius (1 mm in this example) is determined by the global Bend Radius that we sent in the Sheet Metal Properties by editing the Sheet-Metal folder. As a result, all Edge Flanges will automatically use the default Bend Radius value.

However, it is also possible to override the default Bend Radius for individual Edge Flanges. To do this, complete the following steps:

I.   Uncheck the **Use default radius** checkbox and set the required value.

II.   Try adjusting this Bend Radius value and pay attention to how the Bend Radius of the yellow preview in the Graphics Area also changes.

III.   To go back to the default Bend Radius value, just put a check back in the **Use default radius** checkbox.

7.   **Bend angle**: Next, we can set the angle that the Edge Flange is bent at (*Figure 2.4*, (*iii*)). Try adjusting the angular value and see how the yellow preview also changes to match.

8. It is also possible to set the angle as either *perpendicular* or *parallel* to a certain face. To use this option, first, click in the **Select face** box underneath the angle value, select the reference face, then choose **Perpendicular to face** or **Parallel to face**.

9. **Flange Length**: Another important aspect of an Edge Flange is its length (*Figure 2.4*, (*iv*)). This can be set as a Blind value (extruded in one single direction) or using the different end conditions from the drop-down menu, if creating more complex **parts**.

10. The direction of the flange can also be flipped by clicking on the **Reverse Direction** button just to the left of the **Length End Condition** drop-down menu.

11. Although the Flange Length is set as a dimensional value, the actual length of the flange depends on where we measure that value from. There are three options for measuring Flange Length and these can be seen in *Figure 2.6*.

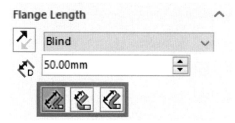

Figure 2.6: The Flange Length options

A representation of the different Flange Length options can be seen from the icons on the buttons in *Figure 2.6*. From left to right, the options are as follows:

- **Outer Virtual Sharp**: This measures the length of the flange from the point where a sharp corner would be if an imaginary line was drawn down the outer face of the Edge Flange and along from the bottom of the fixed flange (the left example in *Figure 2.7*).

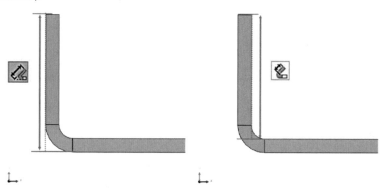

Figure 2.7: Outer and Inner Virtual Sharp examples

- **Inner Virtual Sharp**: This is similar to the first option, but instead it measures the Flange Length from where a sharp corner would be to the inner face of the fixed flange (the right example in *Figure 2.7*).

- **Tangent Bend**: This option measures the Flange Length from a point that is at a tangent to the outside of the bend (*Figure 2.8*). This option is only valid when the bend values are larger than 90°. Otherwise, by definition, the length will be the same as the **Outer Virtual Sharp**.

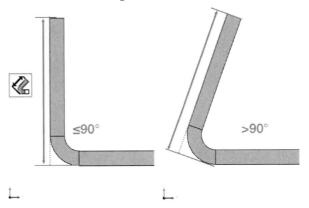

Figure 2.8: Tangent Bend examples for a 90° bend and for a bend over 90°

In practice, it doesn't really matter too much which flange option you use, as long as you use it consistently and your flange lengths meet your design requirements.

12. **Flange Position**: The final option in this section is the Flange Position, and here, we have five options (*Figure 2.9*). In general, the first three choices are more widely used, with the final two being less common, but all have their uses. As with the Flange Length options, the small icons on the buttons give a graphical representation of what each setting means.

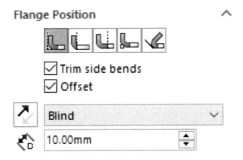

Figure 2.9: The Flange Position options

The **Flange Position** options are as follows:

- **Material Inside**: This option means that all of the Edge Flange material will be inside the area of the fixed flange (*Figure 2.10*).

- **Material Outside**: This option puts the Edge Flange material outside of the fixed flange area, however, it can be seen that some of the bend region itself is still within the fixed flange area (*Figure 2.10*).

- **Bend Outside**: This choice means that the entire bend will be outside of the fixed flange, effectively offsetting the Edge Flange from the fixed flange slightly (*Figure 2.10*).

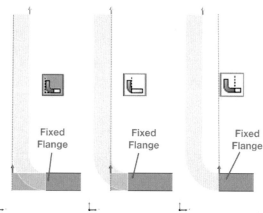

Figure 2.10: The Flange Position options (left to right: Material Inside, Material Outside, and Bend Outside)

- **Bend from Virtual Sharp**: The fourth and fifth options are more specialized and used less often in everyday modeling, but they can still be useful. The **Bend from Virtual Sharp** option bases the bend on the position where a sharp corner between the top face of the fixed flange and the inner face of the Edge Flange would be. In *Figure 2.11*, we can see two different bend angles to demonstrate this. Note that this option can only be used with bend sizes of over 90°.

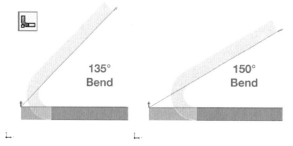

Figure 2.11: The Bend from Virtual Sharp option, with two different bend angles

- **Tangent to Bend**: This option can also only be used with bend angles of over 90°, and it keeps the actual bend face at a tangent to the side face of the fixed flange (*Figure 2.12*). This is subtly different from the **Material Inside** option, which uses a virtual sharp with the outside of the Edge Flange and the top of the fixed flange.

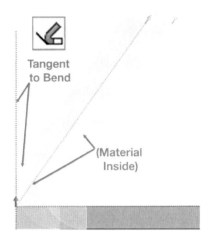

Figure 2.12: The Tangent to Bend option (shown alongside the Material Inside option)

- **Offsetting bends**: All of the bend options except for the **Bend from Virtual Sharp** allow the bend to be offset from the fixed flange. To offset a bend, click to place a check mark in the **Offset** checkbox (*Figure 2.9*) and then set the **Offset Distance**. Clicking the **Reverse Direction** box allows the offset to be flipped and for different end conditions to be selected from the drop-down menu.

13. Set the following parameters, then click **OK** to add the Edge Flange (*Figure 2.13*):

- **Bend Radius**: (1 mm)

- **Angle**: 90°

- **Flange Length**: 50 mm, Blind, Outer Virtual Sharp

- **Flange Position**: `Material Inside,No Offset`

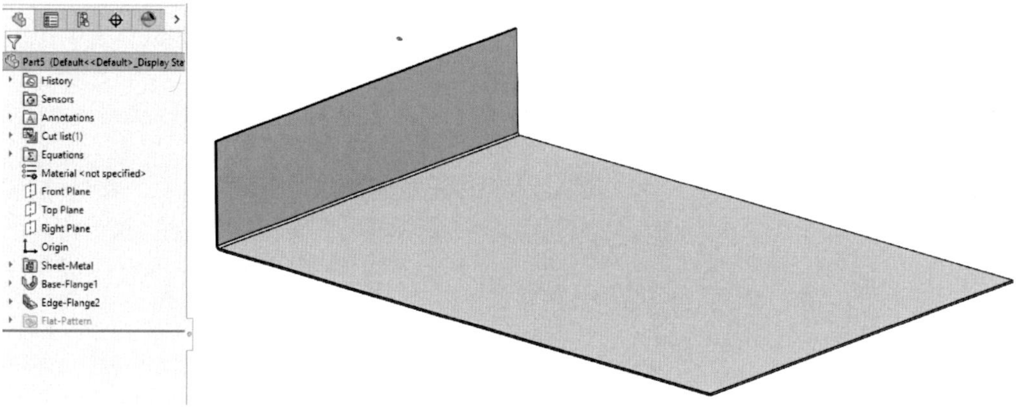

Figure 2.13: An example of an Edge Flange

The new Edge Flange feature can now be seen in the FeatureManager Design Tree on the left-hand side of the screen, and it can be edited in the usual way by clicking on it and selecting the **Edit Feature**.

So far in this section, we have learned how to add a very basic Edge Flange and we have seen that the most important parameters for Edge Flanges are the *Edge Selection*, *Bend Angle*, the *Flange Length* and *Flange Position*.

In the next section, we will look at some more advanced ways to use Edge Flanges and explore some of the detailed options.

Edge Flanges – advanced options

The Edge Flange that we previously added was a very simple example on a single edge, but we can also add Edge Flanges to multiple edges, control the flange profile, and more.

Adding multiple edges within the same Edge Flange feature

It's not necessary to create a new Edge Flange for each edge – multiple flanges can be made within the same feature:

1. Continuing with the **part** from the previous section (see *Figure 2.13*), edit the Edge Flange feature by left or right-clicking on the **Edge-Flange** feature in the FeatureManager Design Tree and selecting the **Edit Feature** option.

2. To add multiple edges, first, ensure that you have the **Edge** selection box selected (*Figure 2.14, (i)*), and then, left-click on the edges where you wish to add flanges. Try selecting the two long sides of the Base Flange, in addition to the one short side that was already selected (*Figure 2.14*).

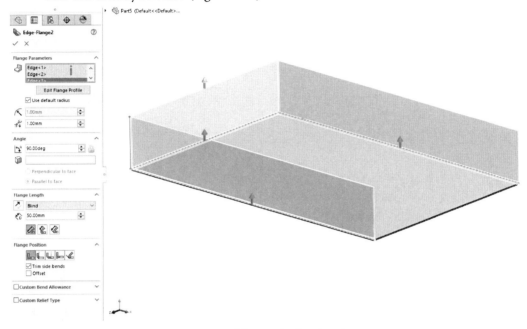

Figure 2.14: Adding multiple Edge Flanges

3. To deselect edges, simply left-click them again in the Graphics Area or right-click on them in the **Edge** selection box and click **Delete**.

4. Click **OK** to confirm the changes. Now, the Base Flange has Edge Flanges on three of the four sides.

Edge Flanges that are over 90 degrees are automatically trimmed

Now that we have an Edge Flange feature with multiple edges, we can look at some more details of Edge Flanges:

1. Edit the Edge Flange feature.

2. Adjust the **Angle** value from 90° up to 120°. This can be done with the adjustment arrows, or by typing the numerical value directly into the **Flange Angle** field.

3. Note that as the bend angle is increased over 90°, the adjacent edges of the flanges will automatically be trimmed back to avoid them clashing (*Figure 2.15*).

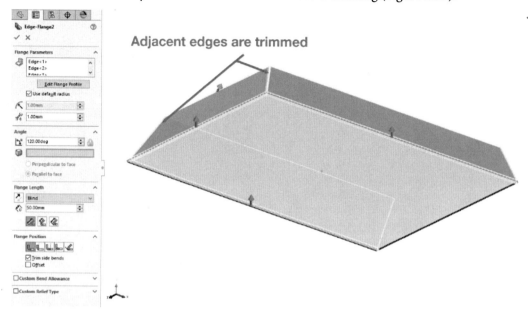

Figure 2.15: When the Bend Angle is over 90°, the adjacent edges are trimmed away

4. Click **OK** to change the **Angle** value of the three flanges to 120°.

5. The **part** can now be flattened to display the trimmed edges more clearly. Select the **Flatten** option from the **Sheet Metal** Tab or Toolbar. You will see that the flattened sheet (*Figure 2.16*) has corners that aren't perpendicular, which is due to the automatic trimming that occurred on the adjacent edges.

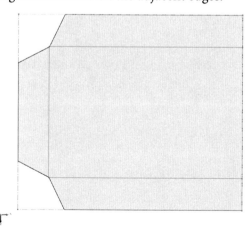

Figure 2.16: The flattened part, showing the non-perpendicular, trimmed edges

6. Click **Flatten** again to refold the **part**.

7. Edit the Edge Flange feature again and reduce the **Angle** value to 60°. Note that if the Bend Angle is less than 90°, the adjacent edges remain perpendicular to the selected edge. They do not expand to fill the gap between the flanges (*Figure 2.17*).

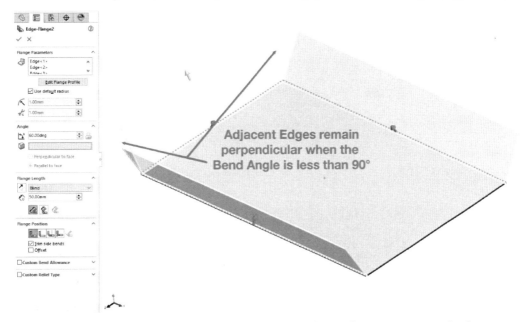

Figure 2.17: If the Bend Angle is less than 90°, the flange edges remain perpendicular

So, when adding multiple Edge Flanges, if the bend angle is over 90°, then the flanges will be automatically trimmed to avoid them clashing, but if the bend angle is less than 90°, then the flanges will not be extended to close the gap.

Adjusting the Gap distance

Whenever multiple flanges are added, we can see that they aren't joined in the corners and there is always a small gap. This ensures that we can unfold these flanges down to a flat sheet correctly.

When an Edge Flange feature has multiple edges, another option becomes available to us. The **Gap distance** allows us to easily set the gap between the adjacent flanges.

Follow these steps to adjust the **Gap distance**:

1. Edit the Edge Flange feature from the previous example and set the bend angle to 90°.

2. The Gap distance option is now available (*Figure 2.18*). Try adjusting the gap size and note how the gap between the adjacent flanges in the yellow preview changes.

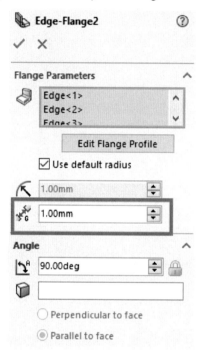

Figure 2.18: The Gap distance option

3. Remove all of the extra Edge Flanges so that only a single one remains. Note how the Gap distance option is now grayed out; gaps can only be specified when more than one Edge Flange is created (otherwise, there is nothing to have a gap between).

4. Select a second edge and adjust the bend angle to less than 90°. Note that the **Gap distance** is now grayed out again; Gap distances can't be specified between Edge Flanges with bends of less than 90° because the flanges are moving apart, so the gap size can't be constant.

5. Adjusting the bend angle to 90° or above activates the **Gap distance** option again.

The **Gap distance** is a fairly simple option that will automatically become available if it can be used. If the bend angle is less than 90°, then the **Gap distance** will automatically be grayed out and unavailable. This is because if the edges are moving apart, a constant gap can't be specified.

Changing the Flange Profile

So far, we have used the Edge Flange tool to create rectangular flanges that run the entire length of the edge that we selected. However, it is also possible to create different flange shapes and lengths by adjusting the **Flange Profile**:

1. Edit the Edge Flange feature from the previous example. Select one edge only and set the bend angle to 90°, then click **OK**.

2. To edit the flange profile, first, edit the Edge Flange feature then select **Edit Flange Profile** from the **Property Manager** on the left.

3. We are now editing the sketch that makes up the flange. A message box will appear confirming that the current sketch is valid. This box can be dragged out of the way if needed.

    The sketch can be edited in the usual way to adjust the flange profile. For example, try dragging the vertical lines inward from the end of the edge (*Figure 2.19*) and adding **Smart Dimensions** to **Fully Define** the sketch. Note: this can be easier from a **Normal To** view.

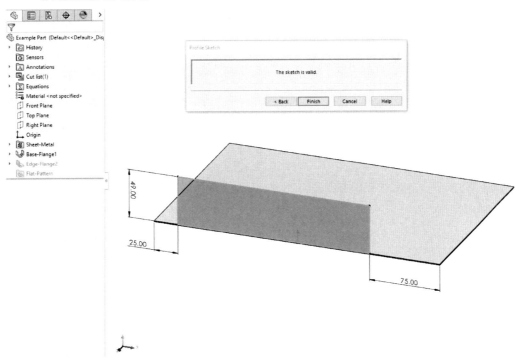

Figure 2.19: Adjusting the flange profile

4. Once you are happy with the flange profile, click **Finish** to accept the changes and you will see that the flange now only runs over a certain length of the edge.

5. If the sketch cannot be used to create a flange, then the popup message in *Step 3* will display **Unable to create the flange from the sketch**. In this case, try ensuring that the sketch has a fully closed profile (with no gaps in the perimeter) and that it is not self-intersecting (it has no overlapping lines).

6. A faster way of editing the Edge Flange profile is to expand the Edge Flange feature in the FeatureManager Design Tree and then edit the sketch above the **EdgeBend** item (*Figure 2.20* – note, your sketch number may vary). This sketch can then be edited as per *Step 3*.

Figure 2.20: Editing the Edge Flange sketch in the FeatureManager Design Tree

7. Flange profile sketches can also be edited to change the shape of the Flange. For this example, the sides of the flange could be angled or curved (*Figure 2.21*). To create angled edges, it might be necessary to delete any existing Horizontal or Vertical Relations.

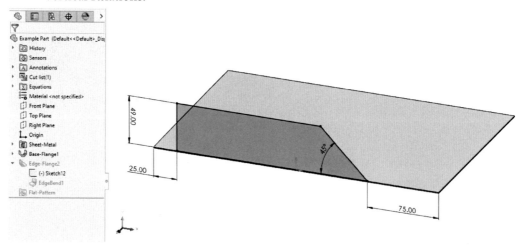

Figure 2.21: Editing the flange profile

Editing the flange profile in this way allows more flexible use of Edge Flanges and unlocks the ability to create many different shapes.

The Custom Bend Allowance and Custom Relief Type options

Two more minor options in the **Edge Flange** settings can be found at the bottom of the Property Manager and they are the **Custom Bend Allowance** and **Custom Relief Type** options (*Figure 2.21*). These allow the global **part** settings from the Sheet-Metal properties folder to be overridden for specific features. They can be used in exactly the same way as the options within the **Sheet-Metal Properties** feature, as covered in *Chapter 1, Sheet Metal Basics – Exploring Sheet Metal Properties and Material Selection*.

Figure 2.22: The Custom Bend Allowance and Custom Relief Type options

These options are rarely used in practice, but they give a little bit of extra control if needed.

The Trim side bends option

The final setting in the **Edge Flange** options is the **Trim side bends** option. This automatically trims away material in corners where two Edge Flanges meet and can be useful for avoiding manufacturing issues that can occur in tight corners with adjacent bends.

This is best explained using the following example:

1. Delete the Edge Flange feature from your current *part* so that only the Base Flange remains.

2. Add a new Edge Flange feature on one of the short edges. This Edge Flange should run the entire length of the edge (just use the default flange profile that is automatically selected).

Set the parameters as follows:

- **Angle**: 90°

- **Flange Length**: 50mm, Outer Virtual Sharp

- **Flange Position**: Material Inside

3. Add a second Edge Flange feature on one of the long edges of the Base Flange, using the same settings as in *Step 2*. You should now have a Base Flange with two raised Edge Flanges (*Figure 2.23*).

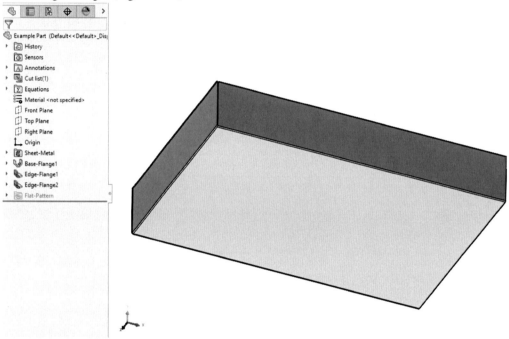

Figure 2.23: One Base Flange and two Edge Flange features

4. The **Trim side bends** option creates an automatic trim in the corner where the two flanges meet. Try editing the second Edge Flange, then, put a check in the **Trim side bends** checkbox and click **OK** to see the difference between the two options *Figure 2.24*).

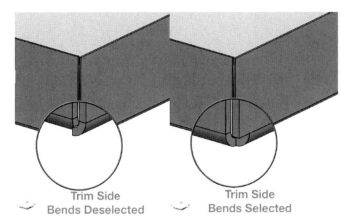

Figure 2.24: A corner with and without the Trim side bends option selected

5. The actual trimmed area is created automatically and has no sub-options; it can either be added or not added.

The **Trim side bends** checkbox is a minor option, but it can be useful for reducing potential manufacturing issues in tight corners.

Summary

In this chapter, we introduced the concept of Edge Flanges, which are some of the most commonly used features in SolidWorks Sheet Metal. After adding a basic Edge Flange, we saw how they can be adjusted by setting details like the bend angle, flange length, and position.

After that, we took a deeper dive into Edge Flanges, and we saw how more advanced options can open up the power of Edge Flanges by doing things like selecting multiple edges and editing flange profiles.

In *Chapter 3*, *Getting Familiar with Basic Tools in Sheet Metal*, we will continue building upon our knowledge and learn more of the everyday SolidWorks Sheet Metal tools.

3
Getting Familiar with Basic Tools in Sheet Metal

Now that we have learned how to create **Base Flanges** and how to add **Edge Flanges**, we can start to look at specialized tools.

In this chapter, we'll discover how to add and remove material using **Tabs**, **Cuts**, and **Holes**. We'll also explore new flange types such as the **Miter Flange** and **Hem**, as well as **Sketched Bends**, which can be used to add more unusual bend styles. Finally, we'll learn about the **Jog** feature, both from a theoretical and a practical perspective.

By the end of this chapter, you'll have a full understanding of the basic Sheet Metal tools.

In this chapter, we're going to cover the following main topics:

- Adding and removing material using **Tabs**, **Cuts,** and **Holes**
- Using the **Miter Flange** tool
- Using the **Hem** feature
- Adding **Sketched Bends**
- Creating and using **Jogs**

Adding and removing material using Tabs, Cuts, and Holes

In *Chapter 1, Sheet Metal Basics—Exploring Sheet Metal Properties and Material Selection*, and *Chapter 2, Adding Bends Using Edge Flanges*, we learned how to make **Base Flanges** and **Edge Flanges** by adding material. However, removing material is also an important aspect of sheet metal, and we will explore multiple ways to do this in this section. We will also learn how to add new material to existing flanges by using **Tabs**.

Creating basic Extruded Cuts

There are many reasons why you might want to remove material from your models. These could include to creating screw holes, adding openings for ports or ventilation, or even making aesthetic features such as logos.

The simplest way to remove material is to create Extruded Cuts, as follows:

1. Open your **Base Flange** *part* from the previous chapter, or start a new *part* document and create a **Base Flange** 200x300mm in size and 1mm thick. We will use this to demonstrate Extruded Cuts.

2. Select the face where you wish to make the cut and start a new sketch (either by selecting **Sketch** from the **Sketch** tab or by selecting **Sketch** from the flyout menu that appears when the face is selected).

3. Sketch the profile that you wish to cut. For this example, I have sketched a square 50x50mm, and 20mm from two edges. Remember to Fully Define your sketches by using the **Smart Dimension** tool.

4. Select **Extruded Cut** either from the **Features** tab or from the **Sheet Metal** tab or toolbar, as illustrated in (*Figure 3.1*):

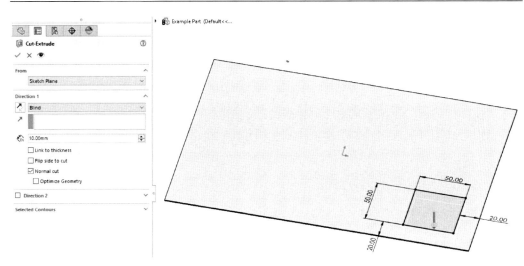

Figure 3.1: Creating an Extruded Cut

5. We can now create a cut using the standard end conditions such as **Blind** or **Up to Next**, but because we are working in a Sheet Metal *part*, some additional options are also now available. These will be explored in the next section.

6. Set the cut parameters as Blind, 10mm, and uncheck the three option boxes immediately below the cut depth (**Link to thickness**, **Flip side to cut**, and **Normal cut**).

7. To create a cut, press the green **OK** check mark.

Linking a cut to the sheet thickness

The first additional option for **Extruded Cuts** is **Link to thickness**. As the name suggests, this option links the cut feature to the thickness of the sheet. This means that the cut will always go all the way through the flange that it is made on. Proceed as follows:

1. Continuing on from the earlier model, edit the **Cut-Extrude** feature.

2. Select the **Link to thickness** option and note how the preview adjusts so that the cut only goes through the sheet thickness—in this example, 1mm. Also, note that the cut **Depth** now disappears, because this depth is set by the sheet thickness.

3. Press **OK** to accept the changes.

Link to thickness is a very useful option for ensuring that cuts are made correctly even if the sheet size changes later. However, there are certain situations where it may not give the outcome that we want, such as cutting across bends, as shown in the following example:

1. Add an **Edge Flange** to the short edge of the **Base Flange** nearest to the cut.

2. This can be done by selecting **Edge Flange** from the **Sheet Metal** tools and then selecting the appropriate edge. Use the following settings:

    -   **Angle**: 60°

    -   **Flange Length**: Blind, 50mm, Outer Virtual Sharp

    -   **Flange Position**: Material Outside

    The process is illustrated in *Figure 3.2*:

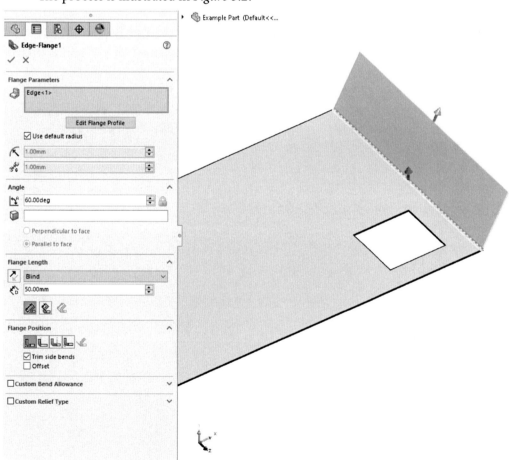

Figure 3.2: Adding a new, angled Edge Flange

3. Now, start a new sketch on the *underside* of the **Base Flange**. This should be 50x50mm in size and straddle the new **Edge Flange** bend, as shown in *Figure 3.3*:

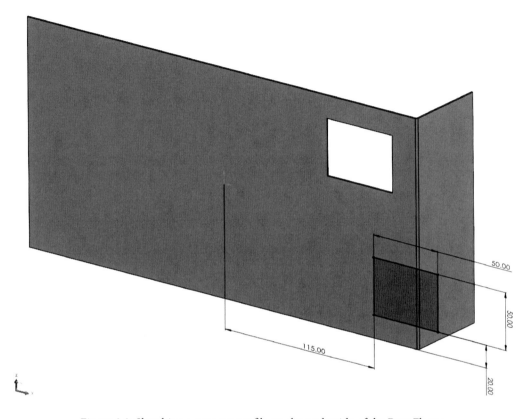

Figure 3.3: Sketching a new cut profile on the underside of the Base Flange

4.   Use the sketch to create an Extruded Cut and select the **Link to thickness** option. Notice in *Figure 3.4* that the yellow preview only cuts through the thickness of the **Base Flange** sheet. That is, the cut only goes through the sheet that the initial profile was sketched on; it doesn't cut through the angled **Edge Flange**:

> **Note**
>
> You may have to deselect and then reselect the **Link to thickness** option for this to work properly.

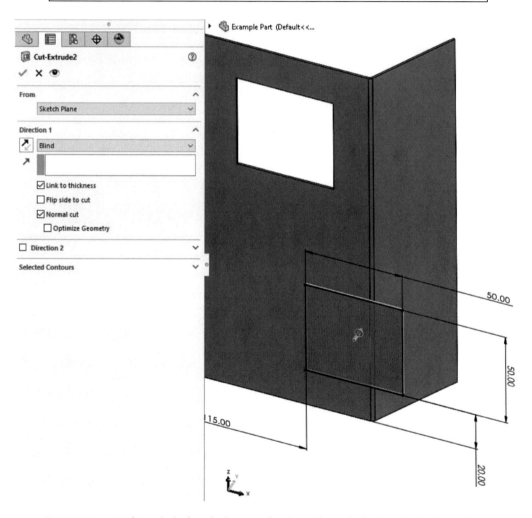

Figure 3.4: A cut that is linked to thickness will only go through the sheet that it is made on

5.   Press **OK** to make the cut.

Creating deeper cuts and using Normal cuts

As well as creating cuts that only go through the thickness of the sheet that they are made on, we can also create deeper cuts. The following example also demonstrates the **Normal To** cut option neatly.

Normal cuts are simply cuts that are made perpendicular (at 90° to) to the sheet face, and these are generally much easier (and therefore cheaper and faster) to manufacture than angled cuts. Proceed as follows:

1. To create a cut that also goes through the **Edge Flange**, we could use a number of different *End Conditions*, such as a **Blind** cut.

    Edit the **Extruded Cut** feature, uncheck the **Link to thickness** box, and set a Blind extrude of 10mm deep.

    > **Note**
    > Ensure that the **Normal cut** box is unchecked.

2. The cut now goes through the **Base Flange** and also into the bent **Edge Flange**. From a Top view, the cut looks correct and just appears as a rectangular opening with square edges. However, if we flatten the *part*, we then see a potential issue.

    Select the **Flatten** option from the **Sheet Metal** tools.

3. Looking at the flattened sheet, we can that the edge of the cut area that we just made now has an angled edge. *Figure 3.5* shows a cross-section view through this cut:

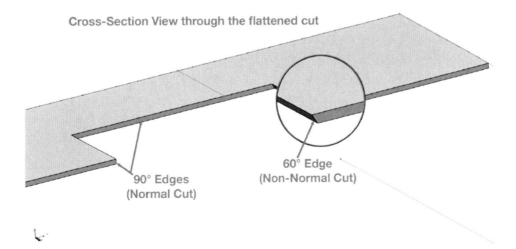

Figure 3.5: Cross-section view through the flattened cut showing the angled cut edge

Note that the edge that was previously folded up now has an edge angle of 60°, which was the angle of the **Edge Flange** when the cut was made—that is, when the part was folded up (unflattened). *Figure 3.6* shows a preview of the cut in an unflattened state to demonstrate why this cut angle occurs:

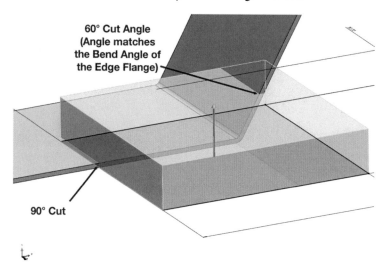

Figure 3.6: Example showing why the non-Normal cut happens

Creating non-normal cuts (cuts that aren't at 90°) in flat sheets such as this can be difficult with certain manufacturing processes such as laser cutting, and so it can add time and cost to parts. To mitigate this, it is useful to be able to ensure that these cuts are normal (at 90°). This can easily be done by using the **Normal cut** option.

4. Edit the latest **Cut-Extrude** feature and put a check in the **Normal cut** box.

5. Press **OK** to create this feature. Note that the angle of the cut is now **Normal** to the face of the **Edge Flange** (*Figure 3.7*).:

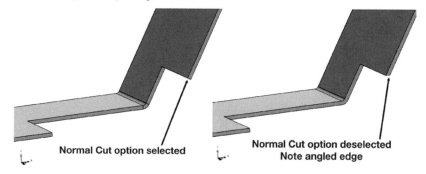

Figure 3.7: Differences between the Normal cut and non-Normal cut options

The **Normal cut** option is a simple way to optimize your models for manufacturing, potentially saving you time and cost.

Cutting Simple Holes

As well as creating specific cut profiles it is also possible to easily add simple holes to flanges. Here's how to do this;

1. Select the **Simple Hole** tool from the **Sheet Metal** tab or toolbar.

2. Left-click to select the face and position where you wish to cut the hole.

3. Edit the hole parameters such as the depth and diameter using the **Property Manager**. The hole depth can also be linked to thickness in the same way as the **Extruded Cuts** in the previous section.

4. Press **OK** to add a hole.

5. To set the exact position of the hole, select the new **Hole** feature in the FeatureManager Design Tree and choose **Edit Sketch**. The position can now be set exactly using the **Smart Dimension** tool.

> **Is the Simple Hole Feature Useful?**
>
> Because the **Simple Hole** feature needs editing to specify the hole position, it is usually faster just to create a normal Extruded Cut, as shown in the previous section, and then to use the **Circle** tool to create a hole profile.

Using the Hole Wizard for holes

If you are creating holes, then the **Hole Wizard** offers a much better solution than using the **Simple Hole** or **Extruded Cut** options. The **Hole Wizard** tool contains a large library of preset sizes and types of holes, and also makes it easier to add multiple holes or edit them at a later stage.

In SolidWorks Sheet Metal, the **Hole Wizard** is used in the same way as for standard modeling. Here's how to work with it:

1. Select the **Hole Wizard** from the **Features** tab.

2. Choose the hole type using the **Type** tab (within the **Hole Wizard Property Manager**).

3. Set the size and end condition.

4. Select the **Positions** tab, then select a face where the holes will be added.

5. The cursor will change to the **Point** tool, and a left click will place *Points*. A hole will be added at the location of every Point.

6. Press **OK** to add holes.

7. To edit the holes, simply edit the **Hole** feature in the FeatureManager Design Tree.

8. The hole positions can also easily be changed by editing the position sketch, which can be found by expanding the **Hole** feature.

The **Hole Wizard** is generally the best choice when creating holes because it contains many preset sizes and makes it easy to add or adjust holes at a later stage.

> **Check Cutouts and Holes with Your Manufacturer**
>
> Many manufacturers have limits on how close cutouts or holes can be placed to edges or to other features such as bends. If you are creating parts with holes or cuts very close to the edge of the sheet or to other features, then it would be wise to check whether your manufacturer has any limitations that may affect your design.

Using Tabs

So far in this section, we have looked at different ways to take material away, but there are also many situations where material needs to be added. Sometimes, this extra material can be created by adding to the flange profiles directly, but it often makes more sense to create entirely new areas. In SolidWorks Sheet Metal, these are known as Tabs, and they can be easily added. Here's how:

1. Looking at our current model with the single, 60° **Edge Flange**, we may wish to add a section sticking out of the side of the flange.

2. First, create a sketch with the required profile. Select the desired face and sketch a Fully Defined profile. In this example, a 50x20mm section is added to the side of the existing **Edge Flange** (*Figure 3.8*).

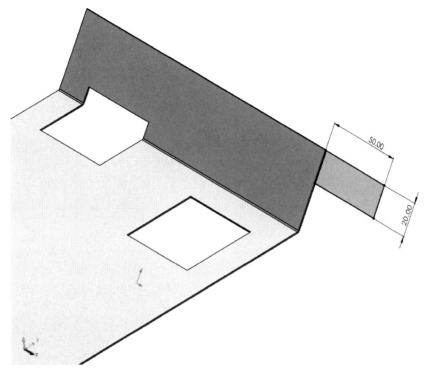

Figure 3.8: New Tab profile sketch

3. The simplest option may appear to be to create an **Extruded Boss/Base** feature using the **Features** tab. Selecting this tool shows that we now have the **Link to thickness** option, but we still need to ensure that the new section is extruded in the correct direction. Therefore, it is better to use a Sheet Metal-specific tool.

4. Instead of the **Extruded Boss/Base** tool, open the **Sheet Metal** tab or toolbar and select the **Base Flange/Tab** tool (this tool doubles up to create both **Base Flanges** and **Tabs**).

5. If needed, select the profile sketch that we just drew, then press **OK**.

    A new tab section is now created and it is automatically linked to the thickness of the flange that it was made on.

Note

The feature is now displayed in the FeatureManager Design Tree as **Tab1**. This is because we are building upon an existing flange so that SolidWorks knows that the new profile should be a **Tab** rather than a new **Base Flange**.

The **Tab** feature is quite simple but is usually the most efficient way to add new material to existing flanges.

> **Using Mirrors, Patterns, and Other Standard SolidWorks Features**
>
> Often, Sheet Metal models are symmetrical or have repeating features. If this is the case, then you can use features such as **Mirrors** and **Patterns** to speed up your workflow. Sometimes, it's possible to create half (or even a quarter) of a model and then **Mirror** the rest of the features to create the other sections.
>
> Tabs, and many other Sheet Metal features, such as **Edge Flanges**, can be used with **Mirror** and **Pattern** features in the same way as standard SolidWorks features.

Adding and removing material is a fundamental part of Sheet Metal modeling, and there are multiple ways to achieve this. When creating holes, it is often best to use the **Hole Wizard**, but other shapes can be cut out using the **Extruded Cut** option. The **Base Flange/Tab** tool provides a fast and easy way to add extra material where needed.

Using the Miter Flange tool

The next tool we're going to explore is the **Miter Flange** tool. This can be used to add flanges to one or more edges and, in many ways, is similar to the **Edge Flange** tool. However, the **Miter Flange** tool requires you to sketch a cross-section profile of the flange, allowing much more complex flanges to be created fairly easily.

To create a **Miter Flange**, proceed as follows:

1. Open your **Base Flange** *part* from the previous section and delete any extra flanges, cuts, or tabs so that just the **Base Flange** remains. Alternatively, you can start a new *part* document and create a **Base Flange** 200x300mm in size and 1mm thick.

2. The most important step of creating a **Miter Flange** is sketching the cross-section profile of the flange. This can be done either before selecting the **Miter Flange** tool or the tool can be selected first, and this will prompt you to select or draw a sketch.

    Both methods produce the same end result and are very similar. In this example, we will draw the sketch first.

3. The sketch *needs to be perpendicular to the edge* where the **Miter Flange** will be made. Therefore, zoom in on the **Base Flange**, select one of the small end faces, as illustrated in *Figure 3.9,* and start a sketch:

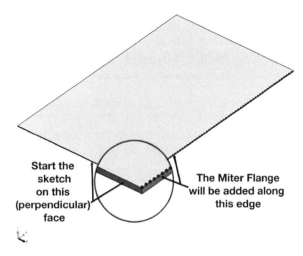

Figure 3.9: The Miter Flange sketch needs to be on a face perpendicular to the edge where the flange will be located

4. Sketch the flange cross-section using the Sketch Entity tools. In this case, we will create a vertical line, 50mm high, in the top-right corner of the face, as illustrated in *Figure 3.10*.

    Note: it can be easier to create these sketches from a **Normal To** view:

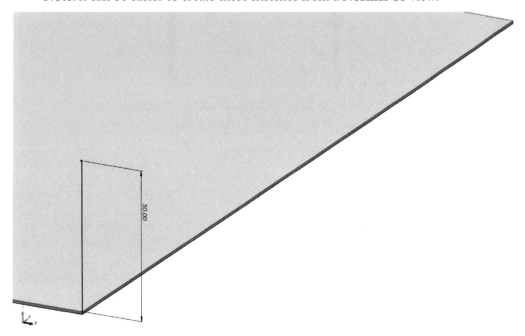

Figure 3.10: Sketching the flange cross-section-profile

5.   Select the **Miter Flange** tool from next to the **Edge Flange** tool on the **Sheet Metal** tab or toolbar. Because we are currently editing a sketch, this sketch will automatically be used for the flange. If we weren't editing a sketch, then selecting the **Miter Flange** tool would then present us with an option to select or draw a sketch.

6.   The profile of the vertical line will now be used to create a **Miter Flange** along the long edge of the **Base Flange** (*Figure 3.11*). If you can't see the yellow preview, then ensure that you have the long edge selected in the **Along Edges** selection box at the top of the **Property Manager** on the left.

The **Miter Flange** can be thought of as roughly similar to the **Swept Boss/Base** tool in normal solid modeling where a **Path** and **Profile** sketch are both needed. In this case, the **Profile** sketch is the vertical line sketch that we drew, and the **Path** sketch is the edge of the **Base Flange** that is selected.

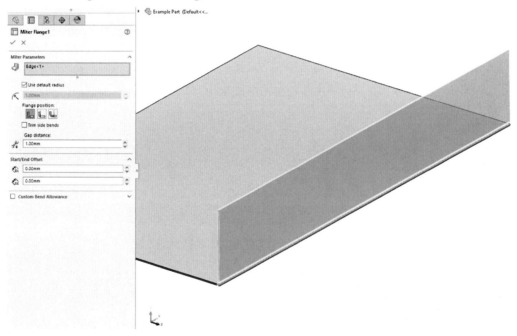

Figure 3.11: Creating a Miter Flange

7.   Note that even though we sketched a completely vertical line from the sharp corner of the **Base Flange**, the new flange preview automatically has the default bend radius from the **Sheet-Metal** properties folder. This Bend Radius can also be changed by deselecting the **Use default radius** box and setting a value.

8. The exact position of the flange can be specified using the three **Flange Position** buttons. The **Trim Side Bends** and **Custom Bend Allowance** options can also be used, and the start and end of the **Miter Flange** can be offset.

9. Press **OK** to create a **Miter Flange**.

Adding multiple edges

One of the great benefits of using **Miter Flanges** instead of **Edge Flanges** is that corners between multiple edges can be mitered. In this context, this means that they join correctly at the corners with a specific gap.

To add multiple edges and demonstrate the mitered corners, proceed as follows:

1. Edit the **Miter Flange** feature in the FeatureManager Design Tree.

2. Ensure you are in the **Along Edges** selection box (this should be blue). If not, then left-click in the box to select it.

3. Left-click on more edges of the **Base Flange** to select them, and you should see the yellow preview now adds new flanges to the edges selected.

   Note that the *edges selected have to be adjacent to each other* and have to connect back to the original edge/face where the initial sketch was drawn.

4. The **Gap distance** option in the **Property Manager** allows the gap between the adjacent flanges to be adjusted.

5. Select all four of the **Base Flange** edges and press **OK** to create a **Miter Flange** feature.

As mentioned, one of the key benefits of using the **Miter Flange** instead of the **Edge Flange** is that it allows corners to be properly mitered:

1. Expand the **Miter Flange** feature in the FeatureManager Design Tree and edit the sketch. We can now change the profile of the flange.

2. Select the vertical line by left-clicking on it, and delete the Vertical Relation. This can be done either by selecting and deleting the small **Vertical Relation** symbol next to the line in the **Graphics Area** or by deleting the Vertical Relation in the **Existing Relations** box at the top of the **Property Manager** on the left.

   When the Vertical Relation is deleted, the line should turn blue, which indicates that it is now Under Defined.

3. Use **Smart Dimension** to add an angle to the line and make it 140° from the horizontal, as illustrated in *Figure 3.12*:

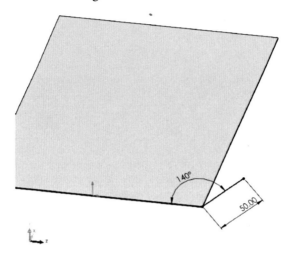

Figure 3.12: Editing the line so that it is no longer vertical

4. Exit the sketch by clicking the icon in the top right of the **Graphics Area** or the **Exit Sketch** button on the **Sketch** tab. You should now see that all four of the flanges are angled outward, and the corners extend to give a constant gap between them (that is, they are mitered correctly), as illustrated in *Figure 3.13*:

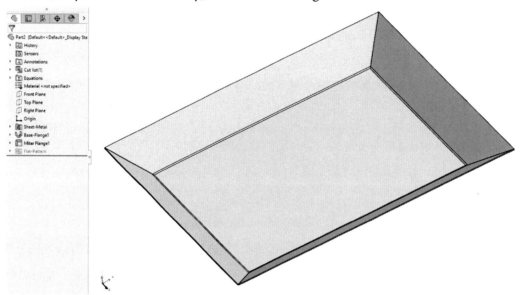

Figure 3.13: The Miter Flange with mitered corners

Creating more complex Flange Profiles

Maintaining the mitered corners of flanges is a useful feature, but the main advantage of using **Miter Flanges** is that the initial sketch can be edited to create complex flange shapes without lots of extra features or work. Here's how we do this:

1. Expand the **Miter Flange** feature and edit the profile sketch again.

2. We can now edit the line and add multiple new lines. Try creating a sketch similar to the one shown in *Figure 3.14:*

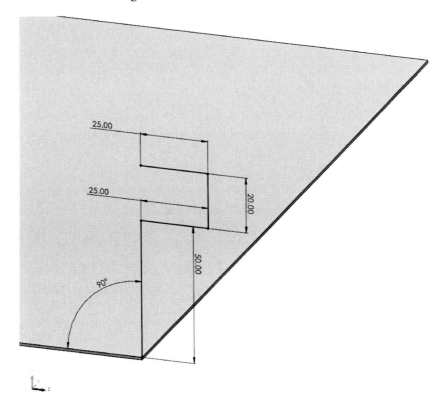

Figure 3.14: Try adjusting the Miter Flange profile sketch similar to this

3. Exit the sketch, and it can now be seen that the updated sketch is used for the **Miter Flange**. Note again that the Bend Radius has been applied to any sharp corners.

This feature demonstrates the value of the **Miter Flange** tool: in this case, we have replaced four potential **Edge Flange** features with just one single **Miter Flange**. Although the two tools are similar, the **Miter Flange** tool provides a much more powerful level of control and allows you to save time by combining multiple features in this way.

> **Make Sure the Bends can Actually Be Made in Real Life!**
>
> Although the **Miter Flange** feature is very useful, it can also be quite easy to use it to create tightly folded flanges on multiple edges that could be difficult to create using real-world manufacturing techniques.
>
> When creating SolidWorks models for production, try to always keep in mind how the parts will actually be made in real life, and adjust your models if necessary.

So far, we have looked at two main types of flanges: **Edge Flanges** and **Miter Flanges**. In the next section, we'll look at **Hems**, which are another type of flange, whereby an edge is tightly folded over on itself.

Using the Hem feature

The term *hem* originally comes from fabric-making and describes material that is doubled up and folded over. Hems can be seen on many items of clothing, such as at the bottom of trouser legs or at the end of t-shirt arms.

The main functions of **Hems** are:

- **Remove or hide edge imperfections**: Since **Hems** fold edges over on themselves, they can be used to effectively remove sharp edges or to conceal cut edges or other defects.

- **Strengthening parts**: Folding the material over doubles the thickness without adding much weight or complexity. This means it can be used as a great way of adding extra strength to parts or unsupported edges.

To add **Hems**, proceed as follows:

1. Open your **Base Flange** *part* from the previous section and delete any extra flanges, cuts, or tabs so that just the **Base Flange** remains. Alternatively, you can start a new *part* document and create a **Base Flange** 200x300mm in size and 1mm thick.

2. Select the **Hem** tool from the **Sheet Metal** tools. This can be found next to the **Miter Flange** tool.

3. There are many different options when creating **Hems**, but the first thing to select is the edge where the **Hem** should be added:

    I. Click in the **Edges** selection box at the top of the **Property Manager** and then left-click on edges to add them.

    II. Left-click to select one of the long edges of the **Base Flange**.

III. Multiple edges can be added in a similar way to **Edge** and **Miter Flanges**, and the **Miter Gap** can be adjusted if required.

IV. The hem width can also be adjusted by selecting the **Edit Hem Width** option and adjusting the sketch.

V. The direction of the **Hem** fold can also be flipped by clicking the **Reverse Direction** box.

4. We can now specify the exact position of the **Hem** using the first two buttons. As with the previous tool, the small icons on the buttons demonstrate each option, as follows:

- **Material Inside** ensures that all of the **Hem** material is inside the footprint of the **Fixed Flange**.

- **Material Outside** means that the **Hem** material is added onto the outside of the **Fixed Flange** and so is outside of the footprint.

See *Figure 3.15* for an example of both types:

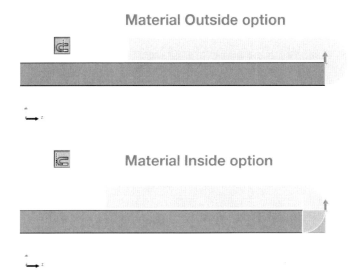

Figure 3.15: Material Inside option (lower) and Material Outside option (upper)

5. Next, the type of **Hem** can be set. There are four options, as illustrated *Figure 3.16* and as usual, the icon shows a simple graphical representation of what these options do:

Figure 3.16: Hem Types; left to right: Closed, Open, Tear Drop, Rolled

From left to right, the Hem types are:

- **Closed**: This option completely folds the material over, almost flat on itself. There will always be a small gap between the folded section and the **Fixed Flange**, due to the need for a very small radius inside the bend.

The only parameter that can be set is the length of the flange, and this includes both the straight (folded over) section and also the outside of the bend area.

- **Open**: This type is quite similar to the **Closed** type but allows a gap distance to be set. Again, the length of Hem includes the bend area. Therefore, a larger gap will have a larger bend radius and so will have a shorter straight section for any given Hem length, as illustrated in *Figure 3.17*.

Note that Hems (and many other features) can be double-clicked to quickly edit the parameters that make them up:

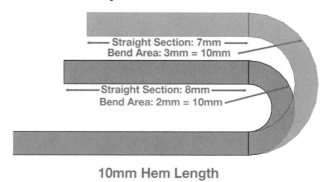

Figure 3.17: The Hem length includes the bend area, so a larger gap will reduce the length of the straight section

- **Tear Drop**: As the name suggests, this option creates a rolled-over Hem, with an angled straight section that creates a teardrop shape. Two parameters drive the size of the **Tear Drop** Hem: the inner radius of bend, and the angle of the straight section. The angle is measured between the straight section of the Hem and the **Fixed Flange** and has to be between 180 and 270°. Try adjusting the angle and notice how the length of the straight section automatically adjusts to maintain the same gap between the edge of the Hem and the **Fixed Flange**.

- **Rolled**: The final type of Hem is very similar to the **Tear Drop** option but simply removes the straight section of material. The **Rolled** option is also controlled by the inner radius of the bend and the angle, but in this case, any angle can be set. However, be aware that although large angles can be used, anything over about 300° will probably result in the material of the Hem clashing with itself, and this could cause manufacturing problems.

6. Similar to many other **Sheet Metal** tools, we can also adjust the **Custom Bend Allowance** and **Custom Relief Type** values for the **Hem** feature if required.

Hems are a very useful little features that are mostly used for improving edges and adding strength. There are four types, and these can all be added to multiple edges in a similar way to other flanges. Now, we will introduce the **Sketched Bends** feature, which allows us to add bends anywhere on a sheet, using sketched lines.

Adding Sketched Bends

Instead of adding bends at existing edges, we can also use sketches to define exactly where bends will be made:

1. Open your **Base Flange** *part* from the previous section and delete any extra flanges, cuts, or tabs so that just the **Base Flange** remains. Alternatively, you can start a new *part* document and create a **Base Flange** 200x300mm in size and 1mm thick.

2. A Sketched Bend starts with a sketch, so select the top face of the **Base Flange** and start a sketch.

    As with many SolidWorks tools, it is also possible to select the **Sketched Bend** feature first. If so, you will then be prompted to create or select a sketch for use with the feature.

3. Use the **Line** tool to sketch a diagonal line across one corner of the **Base Flange**. Make each end point of the line 100mm from the corner of the **Base Flange**, as illustrated *Figure 3.18*. This line will determine where the bend will be made:

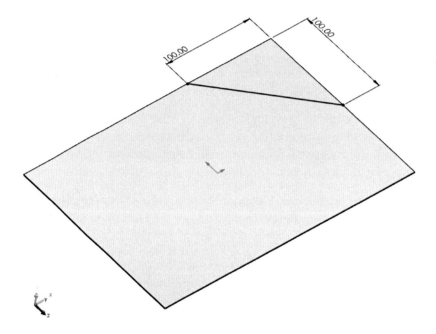

Figure 3.18: Adding a sketched line to define where the Sketched Bend will be made

4. Select the **Sketched Bend** feature from the **Sheet Metal** tab or toolbar.

5. In the **Property Manager**, ensure that the **Fixed Face** box at the top is selected (this should be blue). The Fixed Face is the section of the model that won't move when the bend is created.

6. Select the larger region of the **Base Flange** face by left-clicking. A yellow preview should appear, showing the triangular corner of the **Base Flange** bent up along the sketched line, as illustrated in *Figure 3.19*.

    Try deselecting the **Fixed Face**, then selecting the smaller, triangular area to see the difference between each selection:

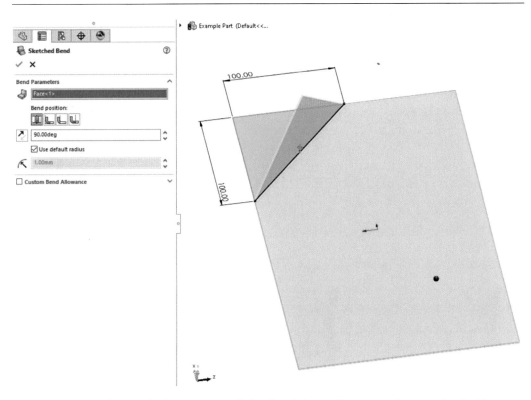

Figure 3.19: Selecting the large region will then bend the smaller region along the sketched line

7. Clear the **Fixed Face** selection, then reselect the original, larger region of the **Base Flange** face.

8. The angle of the bend can be adjusted using the value in the **Property Manager**, and the direction can be flipped by clicking the **Reverse Direction** box. The **Bend Radius** value can also be adjusted if required.

9. There are four **Bend Position** options and all are fairly self-explanatory:

   - **Bend Centerline**: This places the center of the first bend at the position of the sketched line.

   - **Material Inside**: This places the entire bent flange within the footprint of the sketched line on the Fixed Face.

   - **Material Outside**: This places the bent flange outside of the footprint of the sketched line on the Fixed Face (so that the inner face of the bent flange lines up with the sketched line). However, some of the actual bend region may still be within the sketched line on the Fixed Face.

- **Bend Outside**: This places the entire bend outside of the sketched line. This means that the bent flange will be slightly offset from the sketched line, depending on the **Bend Radius** size.

10. A **Custom Bend Allowance** value can be set if needed. One of the benefits of using **Sketched Bends** is that we can ensure that the size of the flat sheet is always exactly correct from a manufacturing point of view. If bends are added to a **Base Flange** using other tools (such as **Edge Flanges**), then the size of the flattened sheet may vary, depending on exactly how the bends are defined. However, by using **Sketched Bends**, we can always ensure that the size of the flattened sheet remains exactly the same.

    In practice, this isn't usually an issue, but if high accuracy is critical to your model and you are using non-standard Bend Allowances, then consider using **Sketched Bends** instead of other flange types.

11. Press **OK** to create a **Sketched Bend**.

12. To edit **Sketched Bend** parameters, click on the **Sketched Bend** feature in the FeatureManager Design Tree and select **Edit Feature**. To edit the underlying sketch that drives the bend, expand the **Sketched Bend** feature and edit the sketch found there.

Sketched Bends are a great way to add bends when existing edges are not available, and are a good way to exactly specify bend position. The following section introduces **Jogs**, which automatically use two **Sketched Bends** to offset a flange.

Creating and using Jogs

Jogs are a specialized form of sketched bend that uses two opposite bends to offset a sheet, making a Z or S shape. **Jogs** can be used to offset edges so that they fit into other parts (such as fitting the edges of a lid inside a box), or to stiffen the edge of a part. They are also especially useful when joining two sheets with a flat outer face. *Figure 3.20* shows two sheets of metal joined using a **Jog** and rivets:

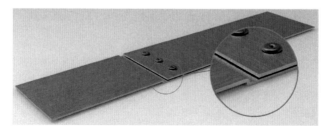

Figure 3.20: An example of a Jog feature being used to join two sheets

Jog features are made in a very similar way to **Sketched Bends**:

1. Open your **Base Flange** *part* from the previous section and delete any extra flanges, cuts, or tabs so that just the **Base Flange** remains. Alternatively, you can start a new *part* document and create a **Base Flange** 200x300mm in size and 1mm thick.

2. **Jogs** require a sketch to define where the **Jog** should be located, so start a sketch on the top face of the **Base Flange**.

3. Use the **Line** tool to sketch a line directly across the **Base Flange**, making it Vertical and 100mm from the edge (*Figure 3.21*).

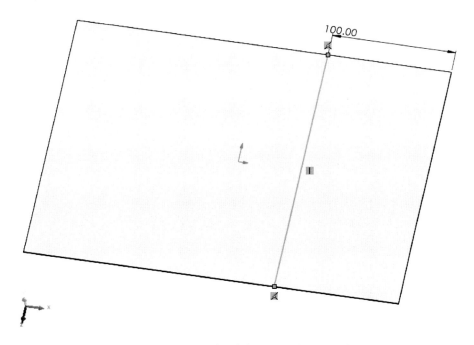

Figure 3.21: Creating a sketch for use with the Jog feature

4. Select the **Jog** feature from the **Sheet Metal** tools. Note that the **Jog** feature can also be selected before creating a sketch. You will then be prompted to select or create a sketch to use with it.

5. Select a **Fixed Face**. In the same way as the **Sketched Bend** feature, this is the face that won't move.

6. Select the large region to the left of the sketch line. A yellow preview will show the bent area. As usual, the **Default Bend Radius** property is used, but this can be overridden if needed.

7. Set the **Jog Offset** property (labeled **i** in *Figure 3.22*). The direction can be flipped if required by pressing the **Reverse Direction** button. Set the offset to 10mm, Blind:

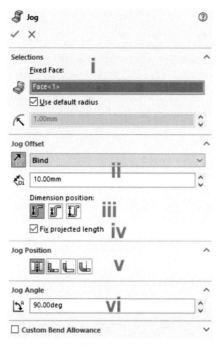

Figure 3.22: The Jog Property Manager

8. **Offset Distance**: The actual height of the offset (labeled **ii** in *Figure 3.22*) depends on which of the following three options (labeled **iii** in *Figure 3.22*) is chosen:

-   **Outside Offset**: This uses the distance between the upper face of the **Fixed Flange** and the upper face of the **Jog** area (*Figure 3.23*, left).

-   **Inside Offset**: This uses the distance between the two inner faces of the **Jog**—that is, the upper face of the **Fixed Flange** and the lower face of the **Jog** area (*Figure 3.23*, center).

-   **Overall Dimension**: This gives the total thickness of the **Jog**—that is, the distance between the lower face of the **Fixed Flange** and the upper face of the **Jog** area (*Figure 3.23*, right).

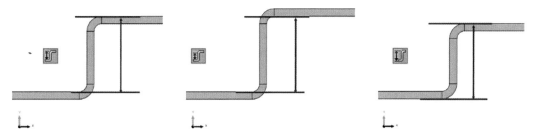

Figure 3.23: Offset Distance types; left to right: Outside Offset, Inside Offset, Overall Dimension

9. The **Fix projected length** option (labeled **iv** in *Figure 3.22*) allows extra material to be added to the flange to compensate for the material that is taken up by the **Jog** section.

    If **Fix projected length** is selected, then the **Jog** flange will be the same length as the original **Fixed Flange**, but if the option is deselected then the **Jog** flange will be shorter than the **Fixed Flange** was (*Figure 3.24*), because some of the material is used by the **Jog** itself:

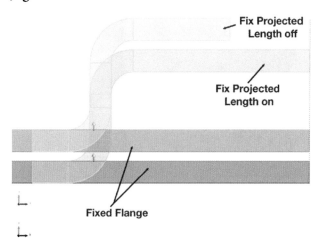

Figure 3.24: Fix projected length option

10. **Jog Position**: The actual **Jog** can be specified in a similar way to the **Sketched Bend** options (labeled **v** in *Figure 3.22*):

  • **Bend Centerline**: This places the center of the first bend at the position of the sketched line.

  • **Material Inside**: This places the first **Jog** bend within the footprint of the sketched line on the Fixed Face.

- **Material Outside**: This places the first bent flange outside of the footprint of the sketched line on the Fixed Face (so that the inner face of the bent flange lines up with the sketched line). However, some of the actual bend region may still be within the sketched line on the Fixed Face.

- **Bend Outside**: This places all of the first Jog bend outside of the sketched line. This means that the bent flange will be slightly offset from the sketched line, depending on the **Bend Radius** size.

11. **Jog Angle**: Finally, the **Jog Angle** property (labeled **vi** in *Figure 3.21*) can be set. Both bends in the **Jog** feature will use the same angle, meaning that the upper section of the **Jog** will always be parallel to the Fixed Face.

A practical example of using Jogs

Jog features can be particularly useful for joining two thin sheets and yet still maintaining a flush outer surface. If two thin sheets butt up against each other and join directly, then it can be very hard to weld or otherwise join them together because we only have a tiny surface (that is, the thickness of the sheet) where they actually join (*Figure 3.25*).

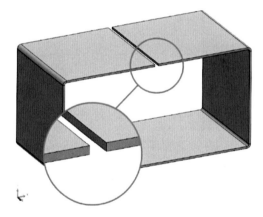

Figure 3.25: Thin sheets can be hard to join without Jogs

To demonstrate how a **Jog** feature can help to solve this issue:

1. Start a new *part* document and create a **Base Flange** 100x50mm in size, 1mm thick, with a **Bend Radius** value of 1mm.

2. Add **Edge Flanges** to each of the shorter edges. These should be 50mm long with a 90° angle, a **Flange Length** type of Outer Virtual Sharp, and a **Flange Position** of Material Inside. Both edges can be added to a single feature. This gives a U-shaped model.

3. Add two further **Edge Flanges** to the top edges of the previous **Edge Flanges** (*Figure 3.26*). These should both be at a 90° angle and have a length of 49mm (Outer Virtual Sharp and Material Inside) so that a rough box shape is created but the ends of the upper flanges don't quite touch and have a small gap:

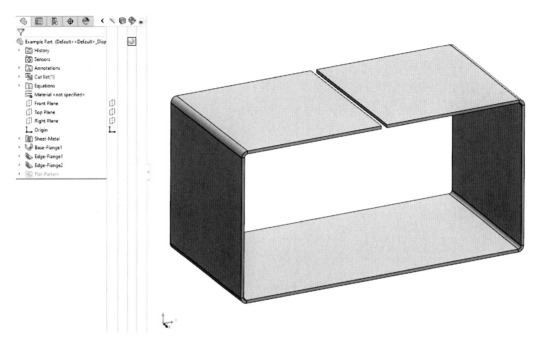

Figure 3.26: Creating a part with a single Base Flange and two sets of Edge Flanges, creating a rough box shape

4. If this part was created in real life, then the unsupported end of the upper **Edge Flanges** would probably be fairly weak. Ideally, we would join them together, but the very thin sheet thickness would make them difficult to weld. Therefore, we will use a **Jog** feature to make the flanges overlap.

5. Sketch a single line on the top face of one of the flanges, making it parallel to—and 20mm away from—the edge (*Figure 3.27*).

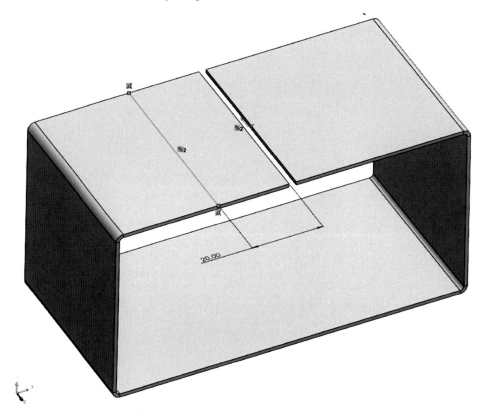

Figure 3.27: Sketching a line for the Jog feature

6. From within the sketch, select the **Jog** tool. This uses the current sketch in the **Jog** feature. We could also have selected the **Jog** tool first, then drawn the sketch.

7. Within the **Jog** tool, select the **Fixed Face**. This will be the larger region of the flange, on the bend side of the flange (the lefthand section in *Figure 3.27*).

8. Input the following parameters:

   - **Jog Offset**: Blind, 1.5mm (toward **the Fixed Flange**)
   - **Outside Offset**
   - **Fix projected length**: On
   - **Jog Angle**: Bend Centerline
   - **Jog Angle**: 90°

9. Press **OK** to create a **Jog**. Note that you may be presented with a message (*Figure 3.28*) warning that the **Jog Offset** value is not correct. Press **OK** to create the **Jog** anyway and we will look at the issue:

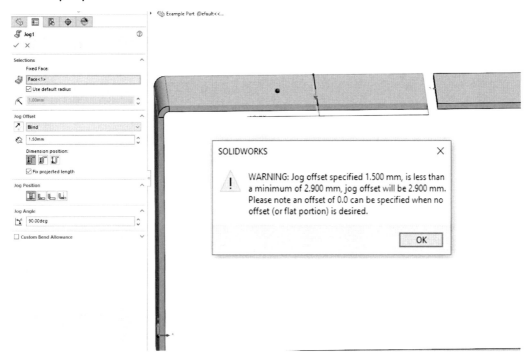

Figure 3.28: Sometimes, the desired offset distance will not be used and a warning will be displayed

10. If we look at the model from the side (*Figure 3.29*) we can see that although we set an **Offset Distance** value of 1.5mm, the **Jog** has actually been created with an **Offset Distance** value of 3mm.

This is because the **Jog** used a **Default Bend Radius** value of 1mm; therefore, the **Jog** is made up of two 90° bends, each of which cannot be smaller than 1mm in size. Adding this to sheet thickness gives our actual 3mm offset.

Therefore, be aware that Jog offset distances may sometimes be different from what you think you have specified:

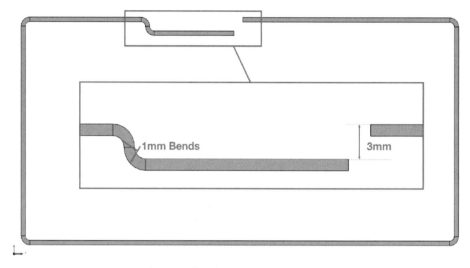

Figure 3.29: Sometimes, the Jog offset distance will be greater than what was specified

11. To reduce the offset distance, we must *either* reduce the **Bend Radius** value *or* adjust the **Jog Angle** value.

Edit the **Jog** feature and reduce the **Bend Angle** from 90° using the down arrow next to the **Offset Distance** box. Notice that as the angle reduces, the **Offset Distance** value in the preview also reduces, because we are effectively reducing the height of the bends in the **Jog**.

At some point (in this case, 60°), the gap in the preview will no longer reduce. This shows us the maximum angle that we can use to achieve the correct offset distance of 1.5mm.

Therefore, set a **Jog Angle** value of 60° and press **OK** (*Figure 3.30*).

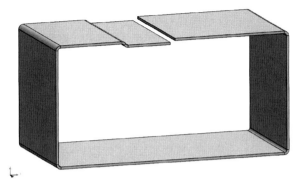

Figure 3.30: Setting a Jog Angle of 60° will give the correct offset of 1.5mm

12. To finish off the **Jog** example, we can now create an overlapping area using a **Tab**. Start a sketch on the upper face of the flange without the **Jog**.

13. Use the **Rectangle** tool to draw a closed profile that overlaps the **Jog** area (*Figure 3.31*).

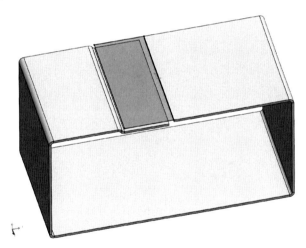

Figure 3.31: Sketching a closed profile on the top face of the flange

14. Use the **Base Flange/Tab** option to create an overlapping **Tab** section (*Figure 3.32*). This overlapping area could then be used with rivets or bolts to join the two flanges together, or it could be spot welded:

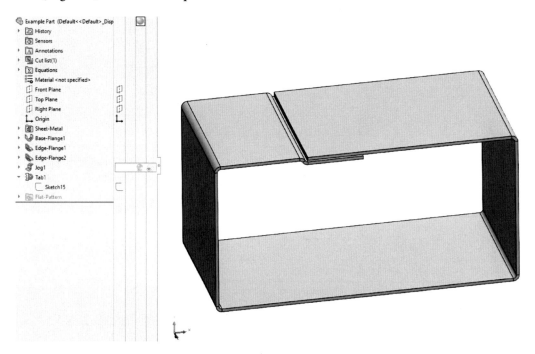

Figure 3.32: Creating an overlapping section using the Tab tool

Jogs are a useful feature that offsets a sheet or flange. They can be used in multiple ways, allowing edges to be stiffened or offset to help parts fit together.

Summary

In this chapter, we learned how to add and remove material using **Cuts**, **Holes** and **Tabs**. We also explored some new features related to flanges: the **Miter Flange**, the **Hem**, **Sketched Bends**, and **Jogs**. These can all be used to add greater complexity and functionality to your parts.

In *Chapter 4, Creating Sheet Metal Drawings and Exporting Files*, we will explore how your Sheet Metal models can be exported for real-world production, and how you can create **two-dimensional** (**2D**) drawings of your *parts* and *assemblies*.

4

Creating Sheet Metal Drawings and Exporting Files

Two-dimensional (**2D**) drawings are essential if sheet metal parts are to be manufactured and used in the real world.

In this chapter, we will discover some of the Sheet Metal-specific details that are needed for SolidWorks drawings, including how to insert **Flat Patterns** based on Sheet Metal *parts*. We will also learn the various ways that Sheet Metal parts can be exported for use, such as **Drawing Exchange Format** (**DXF**) and **Drawing** (**DWG**) file types.

By the end of this chapter, you'll understand how to add Sheet Metal details to SolidWorks drawings, and how to export 2D files.

In this chapter, we're going to cover the following main topics:

- Creating basic 2D drawings of Sheet Metal *parts*
- Using **Flat Pattern** views
- Exporting Sheet Metal *parts* for manufacturing

SolidWorks Drawings overview

Although SolidWorks primarily focusses on the creation of 3D models, 2D drawings are still an important aspect of engineering and product development. After a 3D model has been completed a 2D drawing of it is often created to assist in manufacturing or for record keeping. These drawings can be made from single *parts* or entire assemblies and can range from simple overviews of the models all the way up to complex, multi-sheet drawings that contain section views, detail break-outs and other notes.

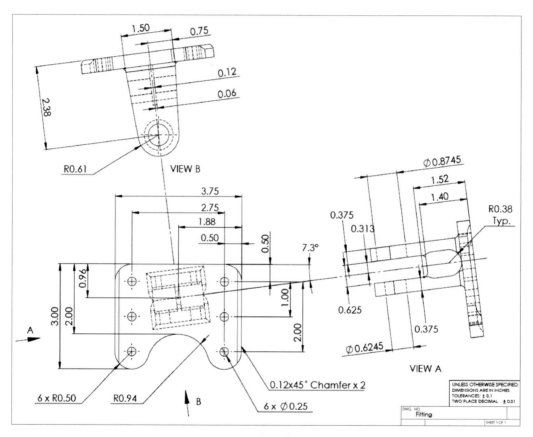

Figure 4.1: An example SolidWorks drawing

The detailed creation of drawings is beyond the scope of this book but as a quick refresher drawings can be created by going to **File | New…** and then selecting **Drawing**.

Various views can then be added to the drawing sheet and dimensions and other notes can be added. When complete, SolidWorks drawings can be exported as PDF files so that they can be shared with non-SolidWorks users.

Creating basic 2D drawings of Sheet Metal parts

Now that we know the basics of making Sheet Metal models, we can explore how we can create 2D drawings that can be used to actually make these parts. Drawings are especially important for Sheet Metal models because sheet metal production processes can often be less automated than other manufacturing methods such as **computer numerical control (CNC)** machining or **injection molding**. An example of a SolidWorks Sheet Metal drawing can be seen in *Figure 4.2*.

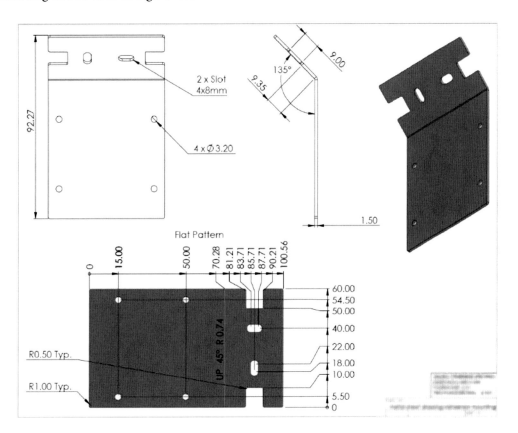

Figure 4.2: An example SolidWorks Sheet Metal drawing

This section assumes that you already understand the basics of creating SolidWorks *drawings*. The chapter is not intended to be an overall guide to sheet metal and layouts (which vary between countries and organizations); it will simply demonstrate some additional Sheet Metal-specific features that are needed for SolidWorks drawings.

First, we will create a very simple *part* that can be used to demonstrate *drawing* details, as follows:

1. Start a new *part* document and create a **Base Flange** 200x300mm in size and 1mm thick. The default **Sheet Metal Properties** can be used, as this *part* will just be used to show generic drawings.

2. Add **Edge Flanges** to all four of the outer edges of the **Base Flange**. Make these 50mm high with a 90° angle. We should now have a simple open-box shape.

3. Save your *part*.

4. To create a 2D drawing of the *part*, go to **File | Make Drawing from Part**.

    It is also possible to create a drawing separately by going to **File | New...** and selecting **Drawing**. You will then be prompted to select the model you wish to make a drawing with.

5. Select a template, if the option pops up. For most users, this step will occur automatically and the default template will be used.

6. We are now in a new, blank drawing and we can add drawing views in the same way as with standard SolidWorks drawings. Try either going to the **Drawing** tab and selecting a view (such as **Standard 3 View**) or opening the **View Palette** on the right of the screen (See *Figure 4.3*) and dragging the views that you require onto the page:

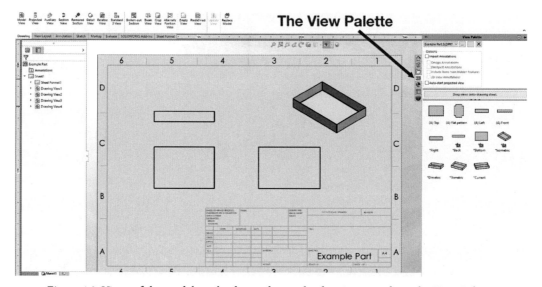

Figure 4.3: Views of the model can be dragged onto the drawing page from the View Palette

7. **Dimensions** and **Notes** can be added as needed, and detail can be added in the same way as standard SolidWorks drawings.

8. **Cut Lists** tables can also be added to the drawing. In Sheet Metal drawings, **Cut Lists** display all of the different sheets that are needed to create your model, and so they can be thought of as similar to **Bills of Material** tables in standard SolidWorks drawings.

   To add a **Cut List** table:

   I. After adding drawing views to the sheet, go to the **Annotation** tab and select **Tables | Weldment Cut List**.

   II. You will be prompted to select a model to use to create the table. Left-click on any of the views (since they are all from the same model) in the drawing.

   III. Set any specific properties that you require or press the green **OK** check mark to insert the table.

   IV. The **Cut List** table will now follow the mouse around and can be placed anywhere on the drawing by left-clicking.

   V. **Balloons** can also be added to the drawing (these are also on the **Annotations** tab) to specify which parts in the drawing views correspond to which entries in the table (they are not required in this case as there is only one single sheet in the model, but this can be more useful with complex models that have multiple sheets).

9. Save the drawing, by going to **File | Save** or by clicking the **Save** button.

10. By default, the file will be saved as a SolidWorks drawing file, but drawings can also be exported as **Portable Document Format** (**PDF**) files and other file types. These can be useful for sharing with people who don't have SolidWorks.

    To save a drawing as a PDF, go to **File | Save As…** then select **PDF** from the **Save as type** drop-down list.

    There are also PDF-specific options that can be accessed by clicking the **Options** button.

Specifying Sheet Thickness

If creating sheet metal drawings, remember to specify the sheet thickness that is to be used. This can be easy to overlook. It can be added either as a dimension or as a separate note.

In the next section, we will learn how to insert **Flat Pattern** views, which detail the Sheet Metal operations needed to actually make the parts from the drawings.

Using Flat Pattern views

The basic drawing that we have created so far is a good overview of the model, but it doesn't really contain enough information to fully make these parts because it doesn't have details of how the parts will actually be folded from a flat sheet. To give this information, we can insert a flattened view of the Sheet Metal model using a **Flat Pattern**.

To insert a **Flat Pattern**, proceed as follows:

1. First, we will add an extra sheet to the drawing to ensure we have plenty of space for the **Flat Pattern**. Click the **Add Sheet** button, which is just to the right of the **Sheet1** tab at the lower left of the screen. You can switch between sheets by simply left-clicking on the appropriate sheet tab.

2. To add a **Flat Pattern** to the new sheet, expand the **View Palette** on the right-hand edge of the screen. If no views of your model are visible, try clicking the **Refresh** button at the top of the **View Palette**.

3. Find the view labeled **Flat Pattern** and drag this onto the second sheet (see *Figure 4.4*). A flattened view of the part—the **Flat Pattern**—should now be visible:

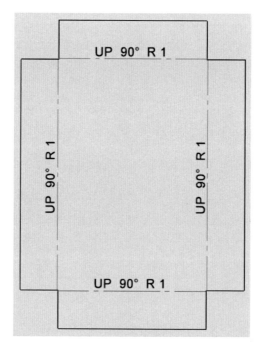

Figure 4.4: Flat Pattern view

4. The dashed lines on the view indicate Bend Lines. If your Bend Lines are not visible, then try going to **View | Hide/Show** and check that **Sketches** are visible.

5. The four notes that read *UP 90° R 1* are Bend Notes. These indicate how these sections of the sheet will be bent. In this case, the flanges will be bent upward at an angle of 90° with a Bend Radius of 1mm.

    If your Bend Notes don't appear, then left-click on the **Flat Pattern** view and ensure that the **Bend Notes** option in the **Property Manager** on the left is switched on. It is also possible to edit the Bend Notes details (and other **Flat Pattern** options such as **Display Style**) here.

6. The individual Bend Notes can also be adjusted. Left-click and drag them around to reposition. The angle of the notes can be changed in the **Property Manager**, and leader arrows can also be added to clarify exactly which Bend Line corresponds with which Bend Note.

Flat Patterns are an essential part of 2D Sheet Metal drawings and can be used to show exactly how your parts will be made.

Using Ordinate Dimensions

When creating Sheet Metal drawings, especially when using **Flat Patterns**, sometimes drawings can become very cluttered because lots of dimensions need to fit within a small area. To help reduce this effect, **Ordinate Dimensions** can be used. These are dimensions that are all added on one single line, from an ordinate (or zero) point.

To use **Ordinate Dimensions**:

1. Within a drawing document, go to the **Annotation** tab, then click the drop-down arrow underneath **Smart Dimension** and choose **Ordinate Dimension**.

Note

The **Ordinate Dimension** tool can be used to add *either* horizontal *or* vertical ordinate dimensions. Alternatively, the specific **Vertical Ordinate** and **Horizontal Ordinate** tools can be selected to add dimensions in vertical or horizontal orientations only. These tools can be useful if you are having trouble getting the general **Ordinate Dimension** tool to pick up the correct orientation.

---

2. Left-click on a point or edge in the model (such as the lower horizontal edge) to anchor the zero point of the ordinate. Drag out the dimension and left-click again to place it. This line will now act as a datum (zero point) where all other dimensions on the line will be measured from.

3. Select further points in the model to add more dimensions to the line (see *Figure 4.5*). When you have finished placing dimensions, press the *Esc* key to stop placing new dimensions:

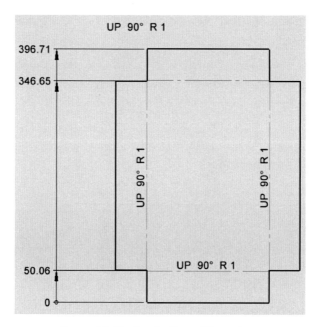

Figure 4.5: Placing Ordinate Dimensions

4. If you find that your Ordinate Dimensions become too bunched up, you can manually drag them around to re-space them. Rebuilding the drawing by pressing *Ctrl +B* also sometimes automatically re-spaces them.

    If your dimensions are still too close together, then try right-clicking on one of the dimensions and selecting **Display Options | Re-Jog Ordinate**.

5. To add more dimensions to the ordinate at a later stage, right-click on one of the Ordinate Dimensions and select **Add to Ordinate**.

Flat Patterns are an essential part of most Sheet Metal 2D drawings, and **Ordinate Dimensions** can be used to make them clearer and avoid them becoming too cluttered with traditional dimensions.

In the next section, we learn how to export Sheet Metal parts in formats that can be used to create real-life parts.

Exporting Sheet Metal parts for manufacturing

Paper drawings are a very useful way of displaying how exactly your Sheet Metal parts will be made, but the initial Flat Pattern will likely be cut out of a larger sheet using a machine such as a laser or plasma cutter. To do this, a 2D file of the flattened part is needed.

There are many file formats for these 2D files, but the two most commonly used are *DXF* and *DWG* files. These two file types are both very similar; they are both 2D vector files that create a drawing from entities such as lines and arcs.

DXF and DWG files can often be used interchangeably, but DWG files are actually a proprietary format of Autodesk (the makers of AutoCAD), whereas DXF files are more open source. For this reason, DXF files tend to be more widely used, and in my experience, they work with a larger range of other software and manufacturing machines.

DWG files can be useful if you are working with AutoCAD (because they contain specific AutoCAD information), but since we are using SolidWorks, I recommend using DXF files.

To export your Sheet Metal parts as DXFs:

1. First, flatten your part from the previous section by selecting **Flatten** from the **Sheet Metal** tools.

2. Go to a **Top-down** view or select the top face of the sheet and go to a **Normal To** view.

3. Select **File | Save As…**.

4. Set the file type as **DXF** by selecting it in the **Save as type** box underneath the filename. **DWG** can also be selected if preferred; this is next to **DXF** in the list.

5. Set the specific *DXF/DWG options*, if needed, by pressing the **Options** button. Generally, the default options will work fine in most situations, and I recommend using these unless your manufacturer specifically requests that you change certain settings.

6. Type in the filename and press **Save** to save the file.

7. Further **DXF / DWG Output** options will now appear (see *Figure 4.6*). For sheet metal parts, the **Sheet metal** option is usually the best choice for the **Export** setting.

Different **Entities to Export** settings can also be chosen. In this case, select **Geometry** (the outer lines of your part) and **Bend lines**:

Figure 4.6: DXF / DWG Output options

8. Press the green **OK** check mark.

9. A preview of the file that will be exported will now appear. Solid lines indicate the model's geometry (i.e., the outer perimeter), whereas dashed lines are the Bend Lines. The view can be adjusted using the controls at the top. If any additional lines aren't needed, they can be selected by left-clicking and then deleted. Note that the usual *Ctrl + Z* shortcut for undoing actions doesn't work in this preview, but there are **Undo** and **Redo** buttons in the bottom left of the preview window.

In this case, we may have decided that we don't need the Bend Lines. Therefore, press **Cancel** to close the preview window. This doesn't cancel the entire save operation; it just takes us back by a single step.

> **Which Lines Should I Export?**
>
> When exporting 2D files for sheet metal, try to consider the end purpose of the file. If the files will be used to cut the flat blanks, then they probably will just need the outer perimeter (Geometry) of the part and won't require Bend Lines. Adding Bend Lines in this case could potentially confuse manufacturers.

10. Deselect the **Bend lines** box, and then press the green **OK** check mark again.

11. In the updated preview window, note that the Bend Lines no longer appear. Press **Save** to save the DXF file.

12. The saved file can now be opened and checked if desired. By default, DXF and DWG files should open using the *eDrawings* program, which is usually installed as part of a default SolidWorks installation.

13. DXF and DWG files can also be opened in SolidWorks by dragging the file into the program, or by going to **File | Open** and changing the file type filter in the lower right of the **Open File** dialog box. This can be useful for using these 2D files to create 3D models.

14. Other programs can also open these file types. For example, a good 2D CAD editor is **LibreCAD**. This is available as a free download online.

    The files can also be imported into **Adobe Illustrator**, and this can be very useful if you need to create artwork such as screen-printed logos or packaging. It's also possible to save models directly as Illustrator files, by changing the **Save as type** setting within the **Save as...** menu.

In this section, we learned how to export SolidWorks Sheet Metal parts as DXF files for production. We also briefly covered different file types and how and why these might be used.

Summary

In this chapter, we learned how to create basic 2D sheet metal drawings, as well as how to use **Ordinate Dimensions** and how to add **Flat Patterns** to drawings. We also explored some of the different 2D file types that can be used to export your Sheet Metal models for production in the real world.

In the next chapter, we will look at a more advanced flange type—the **Swept Flange**—and we'll discover how to use the **Fold** and **Unfold** tools, and why these are important.

Section 2: Advanced Sheet Metal Tools

Now that we understand how to make basic Sheet Metal models, we can start exploring the more advanced Sheet Metal tools. These can be used to create more complex models and can also be used to finalize model details.

This section contains the following chapters:

- *Chapter 5, Creating Complex Parts Using Swept Flanges and the Fold/Unfold Tools*
- *Chapter 6, Utilizing Gussets, Crossbreaks, and Vents to Add Part Details*
- *Chapter 7, Producing Advanced Shapes Using Lofted Bends*
- *Chapter 8, Joining Multi-Sheet Parts Using Tab and Slot Features*
- *Chapter 9, Finishing Off Models Using Corner Details*
- *Chapter 10, Adding 3D Details to Models with Forming Tools*

5

Creating Complex Parts Using Swept Flanges and the Fold/Unfold Tools

Swept Flanges are similar to **Miter Flanges** and can cause confusion with some users, but each tool has a specific use case. In this chapter, we will learn how and why they are used.

We will also explore **folding** and **unfolding** operations. These are distinct from **flattening** and **unflattening** and can be used to make specific features, such as cuts across bends.

By the end of this chapter, you'll understand how to use **Swept Flanges** and the **Fold/Unfold** tools and why they might be needed.

In this chapter, we're going to cover the following main topics:

- How to use **Swept Flanges**
- **Swept Flange** versus **Miter Flange**
- Folding and unfolding

- Why use **Fold/Unfold**?
- Unfolding versus flattening

How to use Swept Flanges

In *Chapter 3, Getting Familiar with Basic Tools in Sheet Metal*, we learned how to easily add complex flange profiles to multiple edges using a **Miter Flange**. The **Swept Flange** tool can be used to create fairly similar parts, but with some important differences.

Swept Flanges can be thought of as similar to **Swept Boss/Base** features from normal solid modeling. Those features require two elements, a *Profile sketch,* and a *Path sketch,* for it to be swept along. The **Swept Flange** also needs these two elements, although existing edges are used instead of a standalone Path sketch.

To create a **Swept Flange**:

1. Start a new *part* document and create a **Base Flange** 100x100mm in size and 1mm thick. The default Sheet Metal properties can be used.

2. First, we need to sketch the profile of the flange that will be created. Start a sketch on one of four small faces of the **Base Flange**.

3. Use the **Line** tool to draw a simple flange profile, like the one shown in *Figure 5.1* Remember to Fully Define your sketch by adding Relations and Dimensions. The sketch profile must be open for it to work correctly:

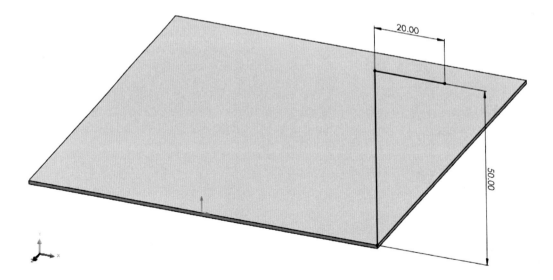

Figure 5.1: Creating a Base Flange and sketching a flange profile on one of the small faces

4. Select the **Swept Flange** tool from the Sheet Metal tools. This can be selected from within the sketch, or the tool can be selected first, and then a sketch can be chosen.

    The message at the top of the tool's **Property Manager** explains how to use it. First, ensure that you are in the **Profile** Selection box (the smaller, top one should be blue), then select the open sketch profile.

5. Next, select the **Path** to be used with the **Swept Flange**—for example, the existing side of the **Base Flange**. A yellow preview of the flange should appear, as illustrated in *Figure 5.2*.

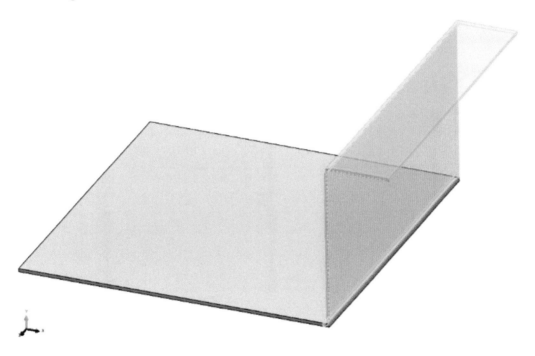

Figure 5.2: Swept Flange preview

6. All of the usual flange options are available, such as setting the **Bend Radius** (or using the default), changing the **Flange Position**, offsetting the start and endpoints, and adjusting the **Custom Bend Allowance** or **Relief Type**.

7. Select the three remaining edges of the **Base Flange** and notice how the yellow preview of the flange continues around the corners of the **Base Flange**, with a curved corner, rather than separate flanges for each edge. Similar to the **Miter Flange** tool, the edges selected must be adjacent and connected to the original flange profile sketch.

8. Press the green **OK** check mark to create the feature.

9.   Flatten the *part* by clicking the **Flatten** button. Note that the flattened shape is very different from how a flattened **Miter Flange** feature would appear if it were made using the same profile.

Because the flat *part* has no bend relief cuts, it is likely that this part couldn't be made with traditional bending methods and would have to use a process such as stamping.

10. Select the **Flatten** tool again to refold the *part*.

Swept Flanges are quite a specialist feature that might require specific manufacturing methods and tooling. The following section will explain the difference between **Swept Flanges** and **Miter Flanges** in more detail.

Swept Flange versus Miter Flange

Although **Swept Flanges** and **Miter Flanges** can appear very similar, one very important difference is that the corners of **Swept Flanges** are joined together continuously—that is, they are not mitered (trimmed in order to fit together). This means that there are no bend relief cuts in the corners (see *Figure 5.3*) and they are rounded.

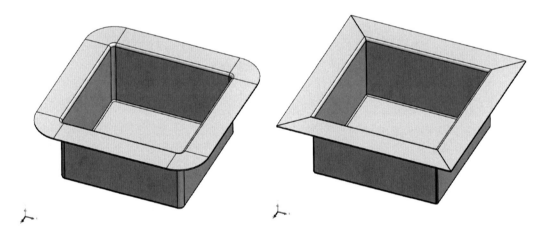

Figure 5.3: The same part made using a Swept Flange (left) and a Miter Flange (right)

The difference can be seen even more clearly in the flattened versions of both *parts*. The version made using the **Swept Flange** (shown on the left-hand side of *Figure.5.4*) has no cuts in the corners and so would have to be made using a process such as stamping and probably would require specialist tooling. By contrast, the **Miter Flange** version (shown on the right-hand side of *Figure 5.4*) has cut corners. These could be created using a generic tool such as a Press Brake and so would probably be easier and cheaper to produce:

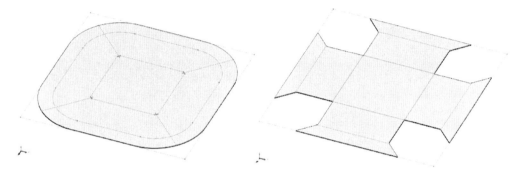

Figure 5.4: Flat Patterns of the preceding models

Both of these tools have their own benefits and drawbacks. They produce quite similar results but with important differences, and so the usage of them will depend on exactly what you want to make and *how* you are planning to make it.

In the next section, we will learn how to use the **Fold** and **Unfold** features to unbend parts in order to add unusual features such as cuts across bends.

Folding and unfolding

Fold and **Unfold** are two related features that do the opposite of each other. As the names suggest, they allow you to unfold bends in your model and then refold them. This can be very useful for making certain types of cuts and other features and will be explained in more detail in the next section.

To use the **Unfold** feature:

1. First, create a new *part* document and make a **Base Flange** 100x100mm in size and 1mm thick. The default Sheet Metal properties can be used.

2. Add **Edge Flanges** to all four of the edges. These should be 50mm high and at a 90° angle and can use any Flange Position.

3. To unfold the bends, select the **Unfold** feature.

4. Now select the **Fixed Face**. This is the face that won't move when the bends are unfolded—for example, in this case, it is the square **Base Flange** in the middle of the **Edge Flanges**, as illustrated in the following screenshot:

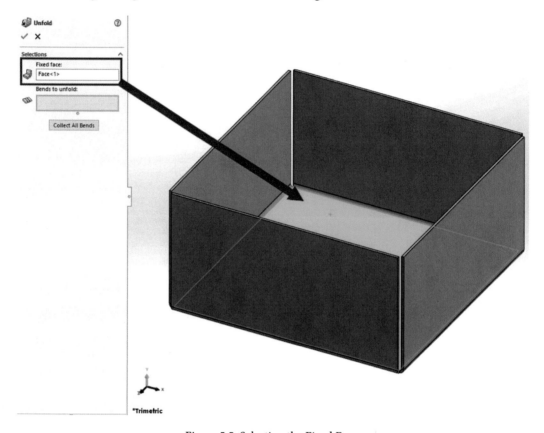

Figure 5.5: Selecting the Fixed Face

5. The bends to be unfolded can now be selected by left-clicking them. Note that you actually have to click the bend face to select it.

It is also possible to automatically select all of the eligible bends in the model by pressing the **Collect All Bends** button.

Select all of the bends using either method.

6. Press the green **OK** check mark to apply the unfolding.

    The **Unfold** feature now appears in the FeatureManager Design Tree. In this unfolded state, we could now make changes to the part, such as cutting across bends.

    Note that the unfolded model looks exactly the same as a *flattened* model would; however, there are some important differences that are explained in more detail in the next two sections.

The **Fold** feature works in the opposite way to the **Unfold** feature—so, all of the steps are reversed:

1. Select the **Fold** feature.
2. Select the **Fixed Face**. In this case, this is the same as the **Unfold** example earlier—that is, the square **Base Flange**.
3. Select the bends to be folded. These can be selected manually, or the **Collect All Bends** button can be used to select all of the appropriate bends in the model.
4. Press the green **OK** check mark. The model is re-folded and the **Fold** feature appears in the FeatureManager Design Tree.

In the next section, we'll explain why the **Unfold** and **Fold** features might actually be needed in Sheet Metal modeling.

Why use Fold/Unfold?

The **Unfold** and **Fold** features can be very useful when making cuts across bends that could not be made in the folded state. Here's an example of how this can be done:

1. Continuing on from the previous model, delete the **Fold** feature, but leave the earlier **Unfold** feature. This should leave an unfolded model with a rough cross shape.

2. Start a sketch on the top face of the *part* and use the **Circle** tool to draw a 50mm-diameter circle that straddles one of the bend areas, as illustrated in *Figure 5.6*. Note: you can use the **Midpoint** Relation along the bent edge to anchor the circle in place:

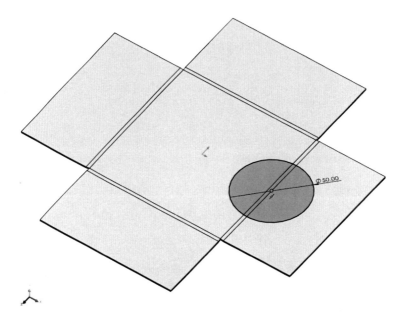

Figure 5.6: Creating a circle sketch on the top face of the unfolded part

3. Use the circle sketch with an **Extruded Cut** to create a circular cut all the way through the sheet.

4. Now, re-fold the part by selecting the **Fold** tool, choosing the **Fixed Face**, pressing **Collect All Bends**, and then pressing **OK**.

This should create a folded box with the circle cut wrapped around the bend, as illustrated in *Figure 5.7* and shows how the **Unfold/Fold** tools could be combined with other tools to make unusual details:

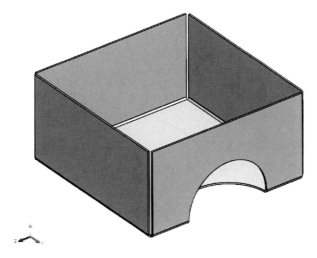

Figure 5.7: The circle cut is now wrapped around the bend

5. To compare this cut with a similar cut made in the folded state, spin the model around and start a sketch on the underside face.

6. Sketch another 50mm circle on the opposite edge to the existing cut, as illustrated in *Figure 5.8*.

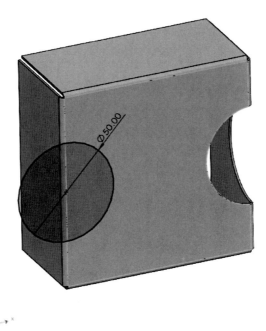

Figure 5.8: Sketching a 50mm circle on the underside of the part

7. Use this circle sketch to create a **Extruded Cut** 25mm Deep, Blind. We can now see each side has a similar cut in the **Base Flange** section, but that the cuts in the **Edge Flange** sections are completely different. The latest cut has a square upper edge, whereas the first one is rounded, as we can see in *Figure 5.9*. This further demonstrates why folding and unfolding might be useful:

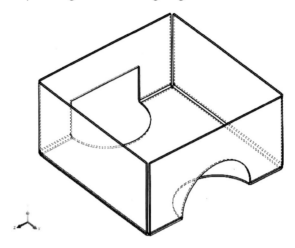

Figure 5.9: The two different cut types produce different results

8. Furthermore, if we now flatten the *part*, as illustrated in *Figure 5.10* we can see that the first cut (on the unfolded model) is completely circular, whereas the second one has two square corners. The first circle would be fairly simple to cut using a drill, but the second one would be much harder without a computer-controlled machine like a laser cutter. Therefore, the first cut might be more desirable, depending exactly on your production processes:

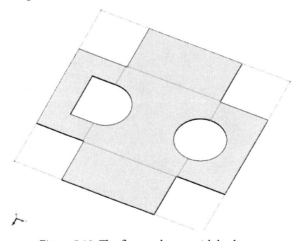

Figure 5.10: The flattened part, with both cuts

It's not necessary to use **Unfold** and **Fold** for all cuts across bends—there may be many cases where it's not needed, but sometimes it can be very useful if specific types of cuts are needed.

In the next section, we will explore how **unfolding** differs from simply **flattening** and why this is important.

Unfolding versus flattening

After flattening the part in the previous section using the **Flatten** feature, you may be wondering how this differs from unfolding. If we can simply click one button to flatten the model, then why would we add the extra steps that the **Unfold** tool needs?

The first, fairly minor reason is that the **Unfold** feature can be used on specific bends only, whereas the **Flatten** button applies to the entire model. However, the main reason for using the **Unfold** feature is that the **Flatten** feature is a special kind of feature, and it is usually the last feature in the FeatureManager Design Tree. When **Flatten** is selected, the feature simply unsuppresses (turns back on) the `Flat-Pattern` folder at the end of the model. This, in turn, flattens the model. When the model is unflattened, the `Flat-Pattern` folder is suppressed (turned off) again, and so any features based on the flattened part will also be suppressed. To demonstrate this, follow these next steps:

1. Using the model from the previous section, flatten the model (if it is not already flattened) by pressing the **Flatten** button. Note that the `Flat-Pattern` folder is now unsuppressed.

2. Sketch a `50mm` circle on one of the clear edges and make an **Extruded Cut**. At this stage, the cut will look very similar to the first cut we made, as illustrated in *Figure 5.11*.

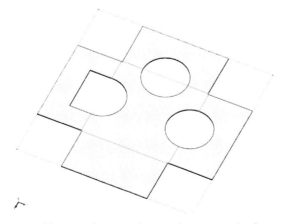

Figure 5.11: Adding another circular cut, this time to the flattened part

3. Now, unflatten the part, by pressing the **Flatten** button again. Notice that the latest cut is now suppressed because it was a Child feature (that is, it was based on the flattened *part*). Any features added to the model in the flattened state will automatically be suppressed when the *part* is unflattened (see *Figure 5.12*):

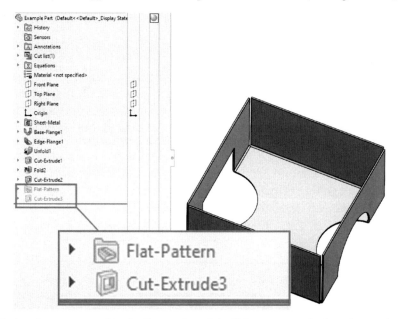

Figure 5.12: Any features created in the flattened model will be suppressed when the part is unflattened

Flatten is only really used at the end of modeling when you're flattening for production or checking that all of your features will work correctly with a flat sheet. Ideally, no features should be added after the `Flat-Pattern` folder, and the **Unfold/Fold** features should be used instead.

However, there are rare cases where certain items—such as holes, perhaps—might be added at the end of the FeatureManager Design Tree, depending on exactly what you're making and your design process.

Unfold/Fold and **Flatten** are two distinct features that each have their own uses, as described previously.

Summary

In this chapter, we learned how to use **Swept Flanges** and how these differ from **Miter Flanges** because they make mitered cuts in the corners. We also looked at the **Fold** and **Unfold** tools, which can be used to unfold bends to add cuts and other features.

In *Chapter 6, Utilizing Gussets, Cross Breaks, and Vents to Add Part Details*, we will continue exploring the more advanced tools of SolidWorks Sheet Metal.

6

Utilizing Gussets, Cross Breaks, and Vents to Add Part Details

Gussets and **Cross Breaks** are common sheet metal features that are used to improve various properties of sheet metal parts, such as strength or stiffness. This chapter will explain each feature in turn – how to use them and why and where they might be used. We will also cover Vents: another common feature in sheet metal parts that are used for many reasons, including to add cooling, access ports, and to create modular products.

By the end of this chapter, you'll understand how to use Gussets and Cross Breaks, as well as how to add and modify Vents.

In this chapter, we're going to cover the following main topics:

- Working with Gussets
- Using Cross Breaks
- Using Vents

Working with Gussets

Now that we have learned about a few of the standard Sheet Metal tools, we can move on to the more specialist tools. The first of these is the **Gusset**. Similar to the **Hem** tool, this is a term that originally comes from clothing. Many items, such as shirts, contain gussets. These are small pieces of extra fabric, usually triangular, that are used to add extra strength. These might be found at the bottom of a shirt at its sides or in the armpit area, or even in the crotch of trousers.

In sheet metal, gussets are also used to add strength. However, there are different things that the term gusset may refer to. Sometimes, "gusset" or "gusset plate" is used to mean an extra piece of metal that is added to an assembly to give strength, such as at the bottom of a post, as shown in *Figure 6.1*.

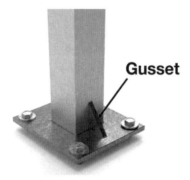

Figure 6.1: A gusset at the bottom of a metal post

However, in SolidWorks Sheet Metal, the term gusset has a different meaning and refers to a ridge that is indented across a bend to give it extra strength. This kind of gussets are shown in *Figure 6.2*.

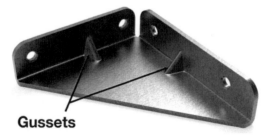

Figure 6.2: A gusset within the context of SolidWorks Sheet Metal

Be aware that although you may be referring to a SolidWorks-style gusset, your manufacturer may have a different item in mind.

We will now look at how Gussets can be used within SolidWorks Sheet Metal.

Adding Gussets

The **Gusset** tool has a lot of options, so it may appear daunting. However, if we work through the options step by step, then it is much simpler than it first appears.

To add a **Gusset**:

1. Start a new *part* document and create a **Base Flange** 100x100mm in size and 1mm thick. The default Sheet Metal properties can be used.

2. Add an **Edge Flange** to one edge. This could be any angle and size but for this example, we will make it 40mm high and at a 90° angle.

3. Now, we can place our **Gusset** by selecting the **Sheet Metal Gusset** tool.

4. As we mentioned previously, the Property Manager looks very complex but follows quite a logical process. First, we need to select the bend where the **Gusset** will be placed.

5. Hover over the **Supporting faces** box (color-coded in light blue) at the top of the Property Manager (*Figure 6.3*). You will be shown a message stating **Select a bend face or two flat faces**.

6. Now, we can place our **Gusset** either by selecting the bend itself (inside or outside) or by selecting two of the flat faces connected to the bend. Note that we can *either* select either of the inside faces, or both outside faces, but not a combination of the two.

7. Select the bend and a preview of our **Gusset** will appear. Note that we can select either a **Partial preview** or **Full preview** using the options at the bottom of the Property Manager:

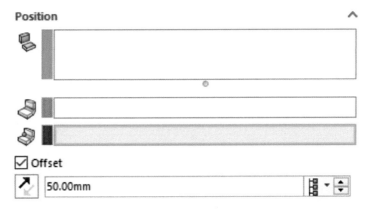

Figure 6.3: Sheet Metal Gusset properties – the Gusset's position

The **Reference line** of our **Gusset** is the next box down (*Figure 6.3*) and is color-coded in pink (note the pink line on the model in the Graphics Area). This will automatically be filled by the edge of the selected bend. This means that, by default, our **Gusset** will be perpendicular to the bend. However, if required, it is possible to sketch a reference line (before creating the **Gusset** feature) that can be used in this box to make a **Gusset** that is at a different angle to the bend.

Reference point is the next box down (*Figure 6.3*) and is color-coded in purple (note the purple *point* on the model in the Graphics Area). This *point* determines where our **Gusset** will be placed along the **Reference line**.

This *point* can be placed anywhere, but it has to be an existing position such as the *start*, *end*, or *mid-point* of the line; it cannot be placed at a random position.

It is possible to sketch a *point* (before creating the **Gusset** feature) that can be used in this box to set the exact position of the **Gusset**. However, it is usually easier to select the start or endpoint of the **Reference line** and then use the **Offset** option to exactly position the **Gusset**. If you can't see the **Gusset** preview after selecting **Offset**, then try reversing the direction; an incorrect direction will mean that the **Gusset** will be floating in space, which means it can't be made or previewed.

8. Select the **Offset** option and set the distance to 50mm so that our **Gusset** is halfway along the bend (*Figure 6.4*):

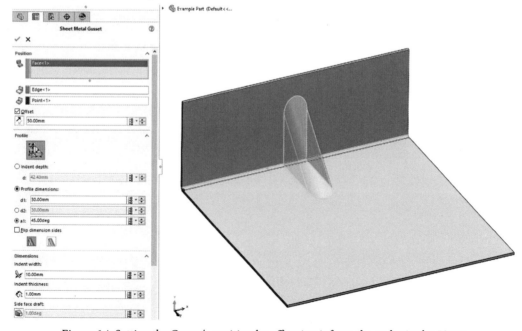

Figure 6.4: Setting the Gusset's position by offsetting it from the endpoint by 50mm

9. The size of the **Gusset** profile can now be set using the **Profile** section of the Property Manager (*Figure 6.5*). There are two main ways to set the size:

   • **Indent depth** is demonstrated by the diagonal dimension line on the large icon at the top of the **Profile** section of the Property Manager. This depth will determine the entire size of the **Gusset**.

   • Alternatively, **Profile dimensions** can be set. We can either set the **Section profile length** (d1 in the screenshot) and the **Section profile angle** (a1), *or* we can set the **Section profile length** (d1) and the **Section profile height** (d2).

   Only two out of these three options can be used at once since the first two values drive the third one.

   If we're using the **Profile dimensions** option, we can also flip the dimensions around by checking the **Flip dimension sides** box:

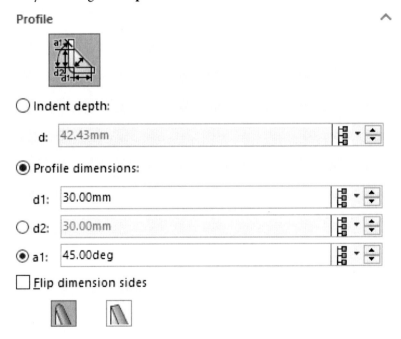

Figure 6.5: The Profile section of the Sheet Metal Gusset's properties

This **Profile** section also includes the option to create a **Rounded gusset** or **Flat gusset**. Generally, the tooling to make gussets is quite rounded, to avoid damaging the parts, but the exact shape will depend on your design requirements.

> **Note**
>
> Use the **Profile Dimensions** option with a d1 of **30mm** and an angle of **45°** and set a **Rounded gusset**.

10. The next section, **Dimensions**, (*Figure 6.6*) allows us to set the rest of the sizes needed for our **Gusset**:

   - **Indent width**: This sets the total width of the **Gusset**.

   - **Indent thickness**: This sets the thickness of the sheet at the area of the **Gusset**. In general, this should be the same as the main sheet's thickness, unless you have a specific reason to change it.

   - **Side face draft**: This allows the sides of the **Gusset** to be angled inwards. It can be turned off completely by clicking the icon.

   - **Inner corner fillet** and **Outer corner fillet**: These options set the size of the fillets inside and outside of the **Gusset**. They can also be turned off completely if not needed:

> **Note**
>
> Set an **Indent width** of **10mm**, an **Indent thickness** of **1mm**, and turn off the Draft and Fillet options.

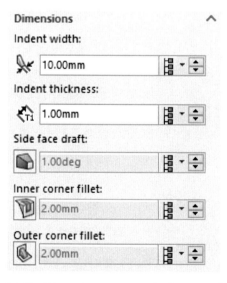

Figure 6.6: The Dimensions section of a Sheet Metal Gusset

11. Leave the **Flat Pattern Visibility** options at the bottom unchecked and press the green **OK** check mark to create this feature.

Our **Gusset** now appears in the model, as well as in the FeatureManager Design Tree. It can be edited in the usual way, or the profile of the **Gusset** can be edited by expanding the feature in the Design Tree and editing the underlying sketch.

Flattening Gusset features

By default, Gussets aren't shown in flattened *parts*. This is because they are usually added as separate processes using specialist tooling. If we want to show Gussets in a **Flat Pattern**, then we need to override the default settings:

1. Click on **Flatten** (on the **Sheet Metal** tab or toolbar). Note that the **Gusset** feature doesn't appear anywhere in the **Flat Pattern** view.

2. Click on **Flatten** again to re-fold the model.

3. Edit the **Gusset** feature.

4. Scroll to the bottom of the Property Manager and check the **Override document settings** box. Then, select both the **Show profile** and **Show center** options and press **OK**.

5. **Flatten** the part again.

   Note that the **Gusset** feature's position now appears. The slot profile represents the shape of the **Gusset** feature, and the *point* is the position of the center of the **Gusset** feature.

   This option will only show the general shape of the **Gusset** feature, so it is recommended to also write a note on the 2D *drawing* that specifies its exact size.

In summary, Gussets give strength to bends. They can be added by selecting the **Sheet Metal Gusset** tool, then choosing the bend, setting the **Gusset** position, and then specifying the profile and size. In the next section, we will look at using Cross Breaks to add strength in a different way.

Using Cross Breaks

Cross Breaks are common in sheet metal and describe a slight bend that's added to a flat sheet to make it more rigid and give it strength. These Cross Breaks can often be seen on the sides of things such as sheet metal air ducts, and they commonly take the form of two overlapping bends that form a cross, or X shape, on the otherwise flat surface. *Figure 6.7* shows an example of Cross Breaks on the side of a metal duct:

Figure 6.7: An example of a piece of ducting with X-shaped Cross Breaks

Cross Breaks are very simple to add in SolidWorks Sheet Metal:

1. Start a new *part* document and create a **Base Flange** 100x100mm in size and 1mm thick. The default Sheet Metal properties can be used.

2. Select the **Cross Break** tool.

3. Now, left-click to select the face where you want to add the **Cross Break** feature. A yellow preview will appear, showing where the **Cross Break** feature's bends will be added (*Figure 6.8*):

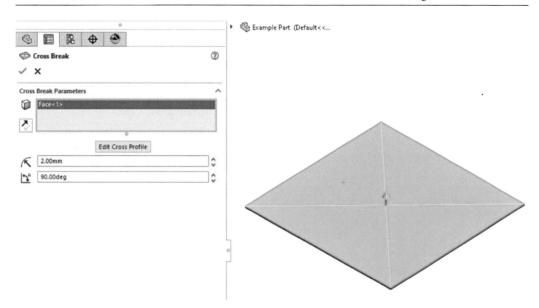

Figure 6.8: The Cross Break tool

4. Press the green **OK** check mark to add the **Cross Break** feature. Note that Cross Breaks *are purely visual features* in SolidWorks Sheet Metal. They just represent where the **Cross Break** feature would be added in real life. The actual geometry of the model is unchanged and it remains a completely flat sheet.

5. Edit the **Cross Break** feature again by clicking on it in the FeatureManager Design Tree and pressing **Edit Feature**.

6. If required, we can adjust the **Break Radius** and **Break Angle** properties and adjust the direction of the **Cross Break** feature. Note that changing these values doesn't change the yellow preview or what the **Cross Break** feature looks like in the 3D model. These values will only appear in the Bend Notes of the 2D *drawing* of the *part*.

7. Cross Breaks are often made in a cross or X-shape, but it's also possible to adjust their profiles.

    To do this, click the **Edit Cross Profile** button from within the **Cross Break** Property Manager. We can now edit the **Cross Break** sketch and a message will appear saying that the current sketch is valid for use with the **Cross Break** feature. The construction lines in the sketch can be adjusted to change the profile. Note that you may need to delete Relations linking the ends of the lines to the corners of the face.

The ends of the lines always have to touch the outside edges of the face, and if your sketch doesn't fulfill this requirement, then the message box won't allow the sketch to be used with the **Cross Break** feature.

8. When you are happy with the profile, press the **Finish** button. Then, once you're happy with the **Cross Break** parameters, press the green **OK** check mark to create the feature.

Cross Breaks are very simple features that are used to add rigidity to flat sheets. They are added as purely visual items in SolidWorks Sheet Metal.

In the next section, we will look at creating Vents.

Using Vents

The **Vent** tool is used to create cut-outs of various shapes and can easily be used to add detailed Vents. This feature isn't strictly limited to Sheet Metal and can also be used in normal solid modeling. However, Vents are very common in sheet metal parts, so the feature appears grouped with the other Sheet Metal tools:

1. Start a new *part* document and create a **Base Flange** 100x100mm in size and 1mm thick. The default Sheet Metal properties can be used.

2. To create a **Vent**, we need to sketch to define the size and shape of the **Vent** feature. Start a sketch on the large, top face of the **Base Flange**.

3. Sketch a circle at the Origin that is 80mm in diameter. Note that Vents don't have to be circular; they can use any closed profile.

4. Next, we need to add extra Sketch Entities to create **Spars**. Select the **Offset Entities** tool from the **Sketch** tab, set an **Offset** of 10mm, and select the original 80mm circle that we drew. This should create a new circle that's 10mm smaller than the 80mm circle (*Figure 6.9*).

    Note that you may need to select the **Reverse** box to ensure that the **Offset** circle is within the original circle. Also, ensure that the **Construction Geometry** options are deselected so that both the original (**Base**) circle and the **Offset** circle are solid lines, not construction lines:

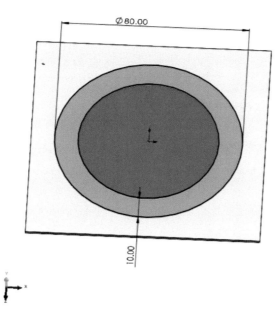

Figure 6.9: Offsetting the 80mm circle to create another, smaller, concentric circle

5. Use the **Offset Entities** tool twice more to add two more circles, each 10mm smaller than the previous one (*Figure 6.10*):

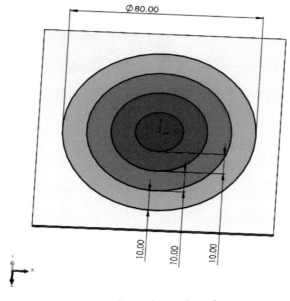

Figure 6.10: Offsetting two more circles so that we have four concentric circles in total

6. Next, we need to sketch some **Ribs**. Note that not all Vents need **Ribs** (or **Spars**) and that the tool can be used with just a simple outer profile if required.

    Select the **Line** tool and add a single, vertical line from the center of the circle that goes out to the largest circle.

7. Now, we can use a **Circular Sketch Pattern** to add more **Ribs**. On the **Sketch** tab, click on the dropdown arrow next to the **Linear Sketch Pattern** tool and select **Circular Sketch Pattern**.

    Select the vertical line as the **Entities to Pattern**, the center point of the circle as the point to pattern around, and set four instances with an equal spacing and an angle of 360° (*Figure 6.11*):

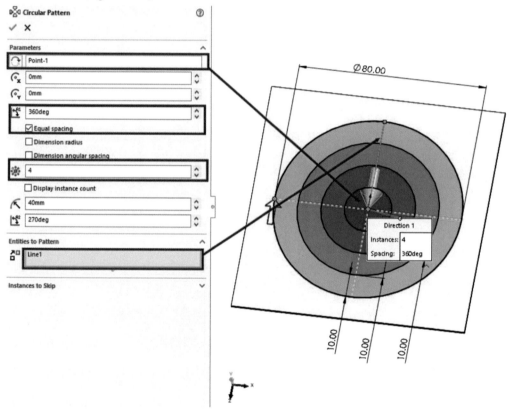

Figure 6.11: The Circular Sketch Pattern settings

Press the green **OK** check mark to add three new **Rib** lines around the circle.

If you are having trouble using **Circular Sketch Pattern**, then you can also use the **Line** tool to sketch these lines manually (*Figure 6.12*):

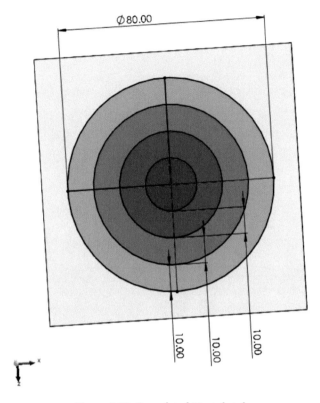

Figure 6.12: Completed Vent sketch

8. Now, we can use this sketch to create our **Vent**. The **Vent** tool can be used directly from within the sketch but in this example, we will exit the sketch first to ensure that no items are preselected automatically, which could cause confusion if you are unfamiliar with the tool.

    Exit the sketch and ensure that you *don't* have it selected.

9. Select the **Vent** tool from the Sheet Metal tools.

10. The Property Manager may appear very complicated but it uses quite a logical workflow. Following the directions provided in the message at the top, first, select the **Boundary**. This is the outer limit of the Vent.

    In this case, select the largest circle by left-clicking it.

Note that a Vent is cut out of the **Base Flange** in the shape of the circle that we selected (you might have to rotate your model to see the **Vent** feature clearly). We could also select multiple lines, for example, if we were making a rectangular shaped **Vent**.

Also, note that the **Flow Area** message now displays **5025.91 square mm** and **Open area = 100%**.

This tells you what the area of the vent is, and that 100% of this area is open (that is, we have no Ribs or Spars that are blocking the airflow).

Under the **Geometry Properties** section, the face has been automatically selected as the face where the **Vent** sketch was drawn:

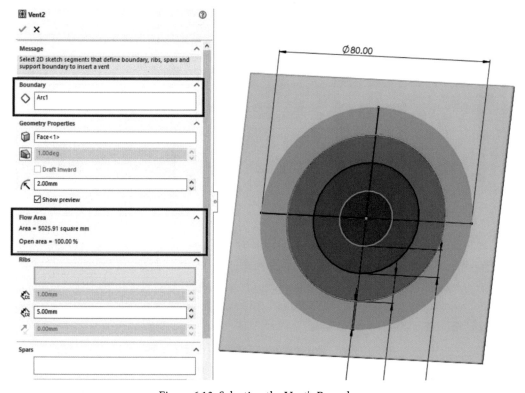

Figure 6.13: Selecting the Vent's Boundary

11. We can now add our **Ribs** by selecting the **Ribs** box and then choosing the four lines in the sketch.

The depth and direction of these **Ribs** will be grayed out as the depth of the Sheet Metal Ribs will always be the same as the model's sheet thickness.

Set the width of the Ribs to 5mm and note that the **Open area** reduces to 84.60%. This is because the Ribs are blocking some of the airflow through the **Vent**.

12. Now, select our **Spars** by left-clicking the **Spars** box and then selecting the two largest remaining circles. Again, the depth and direction cannot be changed, but the width of our **Spars** can be.

Set the width to 2mm and note that the **Open area** further reduces to 73.70% (*Figure 6.14*).

Spars and **Ribs** aren't required in every **Vent**, but **Spars** cannot be added without first adding **Ribs** to connect them to the rest of the model:

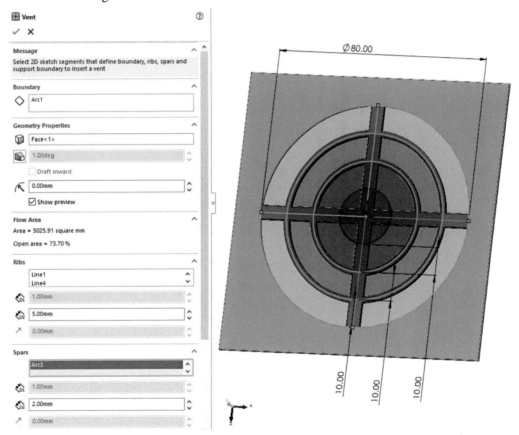

Figure 6.14: Adding Ribs and Spars

13. **Fill-In Boundary** is also optional and is used to close off an area of the **Vent** feature. In our example, select the smallest, inner circle, and note that it is now filled in.

14. Before completing the **Vent** feature, scroll back up to the **Geometry Properties** section. Here, we can set a **Draft Angle** for the **Vent** cuts. This option is not commonly used in Sheet Metal work as it complicates cutting out **Flat Patterns**.

We can also add radii to the joins of the vent.

Set the radius to 2mm. Note that this is applied throughout the **Vent** feature.

15. Press **OK** to create the feature (*Figure 6.15*). Note that it now appears in the FeatureManager Design Tree:

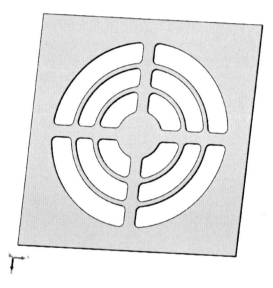

Figure 6.15: The completed Vent feature

The **Vent** feature is not limited to just Sheet Metal *parts* and is very useful for adding these common features to Sheet Metal models.

Summary

In this chapter, we learned how to use **Gussets** and **Cross Breaks**, both of which are used to add strength to sheet metal parts but in different ways. We learned how to edit **Gussets** to produce a variety of shapes and sizes, and how they can be shown in **Flat Pattern** views.

We also explored the **Vent** tool, which can be used to quickly make Sheet Metal **Vents** of different layouts and sizes.

In the next chapter, we will explore the **Lofted Bend** tool, which allows us to create much more complicated styles of bends.

7
Producing Advanced Shapes Using Lofted Bends

A **Lofted Bend** is an advanced form of bend that can be used to create more complex shapes than standard flange types.

There are two types of Lofted Bend—**Formed** and **Bent**, and this chapter covers both, including the major differences between the two.

By the end of this chapter, you'll understand how to use the **Lofted Bend** tool, with both the **Formed** and **Bent** options.

In this chapter, we're going to cover the following main topics:

- Creating Formed Lofted Bends
- Adding Bent Lofted Bends

Creating Formed Lofted Bends

Lofted Bends are used to create a bent transition between two different profile shapes. This can be useful in many different ways, such as when you need to join a square profile to a more rounded profile like a tube.

In SolidWorks Sheet Metal, Lofted Bends can be either **Bent** or **Formed**, and this describes the way the bends would actually be produced. In general, the **Formed** option produces a smoother bend and one that is harder to manufacture, whereas the Bent option approximates the bend shape and is easier to physically make.

Both Bent and Formed types are created using the same tool—the **Lofted Bend** tool, and both start in the same way: with two open profiles. For this reason, Lofted Bends are one of the few Sheet Metal tools that don't require a pre-existing **Base Flange**.

To create a **Formed Lofted Bend**:

1. Start a new *part* document and sketch the first bend profile (see *Figure 7.1*) on the **Front Plane**. This can be drawn using a Center Rectangle, 100x50mm in size, and fixed to Origin:

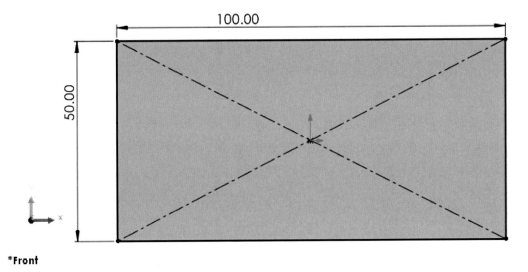

Figure 7.1: Lofted Bend profile sketch

Lofted Bend Profile Requirements

Lofted Bends need *two profiles* in order to be created. Both of these profiles *must be open* and must not contain any *sharp corners*.

Therefore, use the **Sketch Fillet** tool (on the **Sketch** tab) to add 5mm fillets to all four corners, and trim a small gap in the profile to ensure it is *open* (see *Figure 7.2*). This can be done by sketching a vertical Construction Line from the Origin to the top line of the rectangle.

Then, use the **Offset Entities** tool (on the **Sketch** tab) to offset this Construction Line by 1mm (ensure that the offset line is also a Construction Line).

The **Trim Entities** tool (also on the **Sketch** tab) can then be used to trim a small gap:

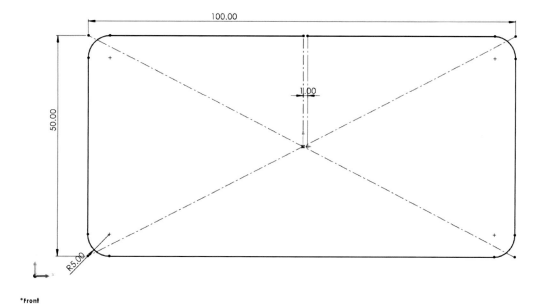

Figure 7.2: The completed Loft profile sketch

Note that the profile is open (it has a small gap at the top) and doesn't have any sharp corners (*Figure 7.2*).

Exit the sketch when it is complete.

2. Next, we need to create a second profile, and so, we need a new Plane. This can be created by selecting the **Front Plane** (ensure that you have already exited the previous sketch) and then selecting **Reference Geometry | Plane** from the **Features** tab. Set the offset distance as 100mm, as illustrated in *Figure 7.3* and then press the green **OK** check mark to create the Plane:

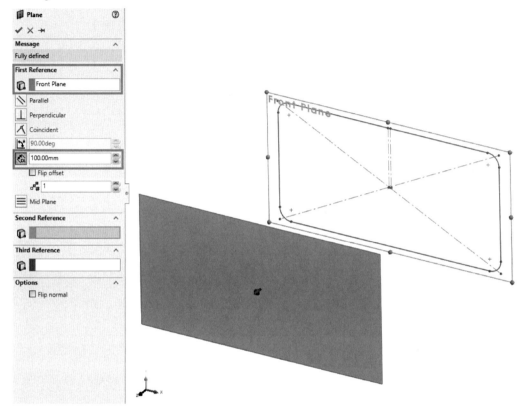

Figure 7.3: Adding a new Plane

3. Start a new sketch on the new Plane and draw the second Loft profile. This will be similar to the first but have a slightly different shape.

    This time, use a **Centerpoint Straight Slot** (within the **Slot** tool) fixed at the Origin, and make it 100x50mm in size.

    As before, the profile *must be open and with no sharp corners*. Due to the slot shape, we don't have any sharp corners, but the slot is still a closed profile. Therefore, we need to trim away another small section, by offsetting a vertical line then trimming a gap, as we did with the first profile. Note that you may be shown a warning message about destroying the slot entity when trimming. This is normal and can be ignored by pressing **OK**.

If your sketch loses its Relations and becomes Underdefined, then it can be Fully Defined by adding more Relations and Dimensions (you may need to re-anchor the slot to the Origin and add Tangent Relations between the curved and straight sections). The finished sketch is shown in *Figure 7.4*.

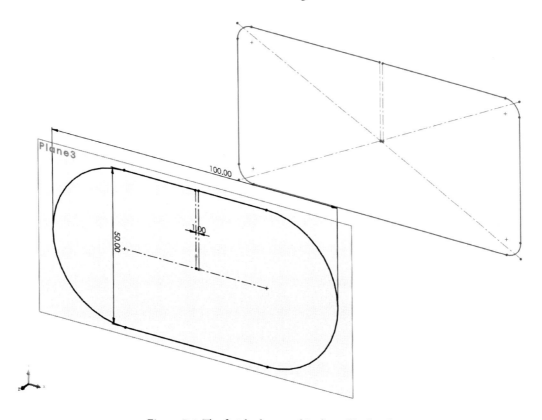

Figure 7.4: The finished, second Loft profile sketch

Exit the second sketch when it is complete.

4. We now have the two profile sketches that are required, and so we can use these to create the feature. Select the **Lofted Bend** tool from the **Sheet Metal** tools. This will be one of the few tools that are available since our model doesn't have a **Base Flange**. If the **Lofted Bend** tool is grayed out, then ensure that you have exited the sketches and are no longer editing them, and this should allow the tool to be used.

5. To create the feature, we first need to select the two profiles. Click in the **Profiles** box (if it is not already selected and therefore blue in color) in the **Property Manager** on the left. Then, select each of the sketches in turn by left-clicking.

Selecting Loft Profiles

When selecting Loft Profiles, try to ensure that you select corresponding points in each sketch. For example, if you select the point at the top-right center of the straight line on the first (rectangle) sketch, then also select a point in the same position on the second (slot) sketch (see the arrows in *Figure 7.5*).

If you are using dissimilar profiles, then it might not always be possible to select points that correspond exactly but try to avoid selecting completely opposite points as this may cause the Loft to twist and make the feature fail.

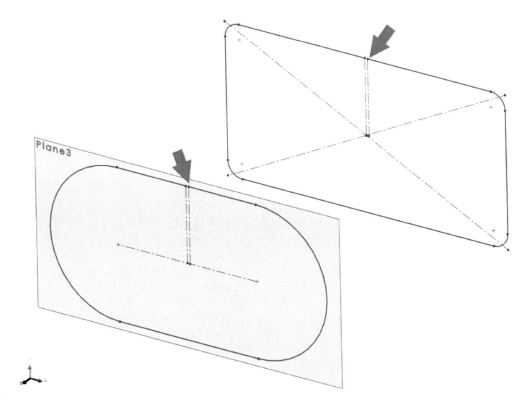

Figure 7.5: Try to select corresponding points on each of the profile sketches

6. We can now choose whether we want to make a Bent or a Formed Loft. Under the **Manufacturing Method** section in the **Property Manager**, choose the **Bent** and **Formed** options in turn. Note that the preview changes slightly with each option (*Figure 7.6*). The **Bent** option has lots of smaller, straighter edges, and the **Formed** option is much smoother.

Select the **Formed** option:

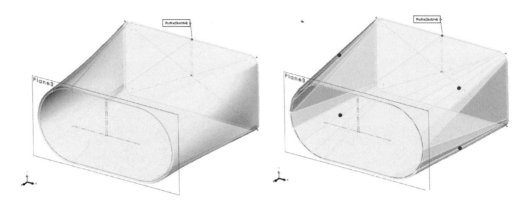

Figure 7.6: Previews of the Formed Lofted Bend (left) and the Bent Lofted Bend (right)

7. The **Formed Lofted Bend** only has a single option to set, which is the thickness of the sheet.

    Set this to 1.5mm thickness.

8. Press the green **OK** check mark to create the feature. The **Lofted Bend** feature appears in the FeatureManager Design Tree and can be edited as normal. The profile sketches can also be edited by expanding the feature and editing the sketches underneath.

9. Flatten the model by selecting **Flatten** from the **Sheet Metal** tools. Note that the flat part has an arch shape, due to the shape of the **three-dimensional (3D)** formed bends.

    There are also no bend lines. This is because the shape will be formed using specialist tooling instead of bent using set points. Because of this, this type of part may be difficult to actually manufacture.

10. Press the **Flatten** button to refold the model.

Formed Lofted Bends are made from two profile sketches that must be open and must contain no sharp corners. Formed Lofted Bends produce a smooth shape but can be hard to produce in real life. In the next section, we will look at creating a **Bent Lofted Bend**, using the same profiles.

Adding Bent Lofted Bends

The second type of Lofted Bend is the **Bent** version. Follow these steps to add it:

1. Edit the current **Lofted Bend** feature; note that because we have already created a Formed Lofted Bend, we no longer have the option to change it to a Bent Lofted Bend.

    However, we can delete the Lofted Bend and then reuse the same profiles to create a Bent version.

2. Exit the **Lofted Bend Property Manager** so that we are no longer editing the feature, then select the feature in the FeatureManager Design Tree and press *Delete*. This will remove the Lofted Bend feature but keep the two underlying sketches.

3. Select the **Lofted Bend** tool, and then select the two profiles again. Remember to try to select corresponding points on each profile.

4. Now, select the **Bent** option from the **Manufacturing Method** section of the **Property Manager**.

5. The **Bent** option contains many more sub-options than the **Formed** option, but at this stage, use the default options and press the green **OK** check mark to create a Bent Lofted Bend.

6. We can immediately see that the model appears very different from the previous Formed version and contains many small bent edges.

    Press **Flatten** to flatten the model, and note that we can now see multiple Bend Lines that would be used to bend the *part* (see *Figure 7.7*):

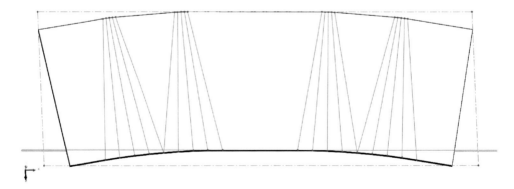

Figure 7.7: The flattened Bent Lofted Bend with Bend Lines

7. Press **Flatten** again to refold the *part*.

8. We will now explore the different Faceting Options for creating the corners of Bent Lofted Bends.

Edit the **Lofted Bend** feature, and in the **Property Manager**, we can see the four choices, as illustrated in *Figure 7.8*. Each of these choices will give a fairly similar output, but the slightly different options allow you to exactly control the bend shape.

Note that some of the options can be a little temperamental with certain loft profiles, so if you are struggling to get the results that you want with one option, then try experimenting with another one:

Figure 7.8: Bent Lofted Bends options

Starting with the first option:

- **Chord Tolerance**: A chord is a straight line that joins two points on a circular arc. When we create Bent Lofted Bends, we are approximating an arc by using straight lines. *Figure 7.9* shows an ideal arc and an approximated version using chords (straight lines):

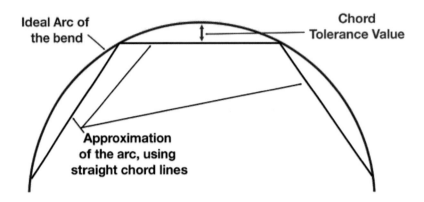

Figure 7.9: Chord Tolerance option

The **Chord Tolerance** option sets a maximum value between the straight chord line and the ideal arc, as shown in blue in *Figure 7.9*.

Try adjusting the **Facet Value** setting and notice how the preview changes. A higher facet value will produce fewer straight sections and so will create a less accurate arc shape but will be easier to make because it has fewer bends.

Note that we can also click on the purple dots on each of the four corners on the model in the Graphics Area (see the right-hand side of *Figure 7.6*), and this will also allow us to set faceting options specifically for that corner.

If you find that when it is created, your **Lofted Bend** has relief cuts that you don't want, then try selecting or deselecting the **Refer to endpoint** option. This can result in smoother bends and reduce problems with these automatic relief cuts.

- **Number of Bends**: This is quite a simple option that allows you to set the number of bends within each corner. Obviously, more bends will result in a smoother curve, but be aware that this will also require more work during production.

- **Segment Length**: This option allows you to set the maximum length of each segment. A lower value will result in a greater number of shorter sections, giving a smoother curve, whereas a higher value will produce sections that are longer in length but fewer of them. This will give a more approximate bend shape.

- **Segment Angle**: The final option determines the maximum angle between adjacent segments. A lower value here will produce more segments in the bend and so will result in a smoother curve.

Each of the four options can produce very similar results, so try experimenting with the settings to get the shape of bend that you require.

It is also possible to override the default **Sheet Metal** parameters here, if needed, such as **Bend Radius** and **Sheet Thickness**.

9. Set **Faceting Options** to values of your own preference and then press the green **OK** check mark to create a feature.

Bent Lofted Bends tend to be easier to manufacture than Formed Lofted Bends but they give a much less smooth curve. The bends can be controlled with a number of different corner types, but these generally all produce quite a similar output.

Summary

In this chapter, we learned that **Lofted Bends** are a good way to create curves between two dissimilar profiles. **Lofted Bends** are made from two open profiles that cannot have sharp edges.

There are two types **of Lofted Bend: Formed**, which produces a smoother feature that is harder to manufacture, and **Bent**, which is easier to physically make, but only gives an approximation of the curved shape.

In the next chapter, we will learn about one of the last major tools, the **Tab and Slot** tool, which allows us to add details to facilitate the joining together of two **Sheet Metal** bodies.

8
Joining Multi-Sheet Parts Using Tab and Slot Features

The **Tab and Slot** tool can be used to simplify the joining of two sheet metal bodies by creating **Tab and Slot** features on each respectively.

By the end of this chapter, you'll understand how to use the basic tool, as well as its many sub-options.

In this chapter, we're going to cover the following main topics:

- Adding **Tab and Slot** features
- Adjusting **Tab and Slot** properties

Adding Tab and Slot features

So far in this book, we have only created Sheet Metal *parts* that contain one single sheet. However, it is also possible to make parts that have multiple sheets.

In SolidWorks Sheet Metal, **sheets** can be thought of in a similar way to **bodies** in normal solid modeling. They are separate solids within a model that aren't connected to each other. They may be touching, but they are still separate solids.

An example of a Sheet Metal model with multiple sheets might be an enclosure that is made from two sections—a **Body** (the first sheet) and a separate **Lid** (the second sheet). Although both the **Lid** and the **Body** are made within one single SolidWorks *part* document, they are both separate elements within that part.

The **Tab and Slot** tool is a great way of connecting two of these sheets together. It cuts slots from one sheet and adds corresponding tabs to the other, allowing the two sheets to mesh together and making it easier to create a join like a weld.

The **Tab and Slot** tool is not purely a Sheet Metal tool; as with the **Vent** tool, it can be used in normal, solid modeling parts, but it is very useful during sheet metal work, so it is grouped with the Sheet Metal tools.

To create a **Tab and Slot** feature, we first need to make a model with two sheets:

1. Start a new *part* document and use the **Center Rectangle** tool to create a **Base Flange** that is fixed to the Origin and is 100x100mm in size and 4mm thick. The default Sheet Metal properties can be used, as illustrated in *Figure 8.1*.

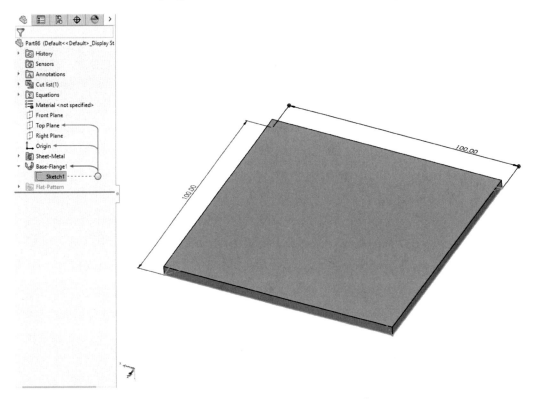

Figure 8.1: Creating a 100x100x4mm Base Flange

2. In *Chapter 3*, *Getting Familiar with Basic Tools in Sheet Metal*, we learned how to use the **Jog** tool to join two *parallel* sheets or flanges together, but if we are trying to join two *perpendicular* sheets, then the **Tab and Slot** tool is much more suitable because it provides more surface area to help join the two sheets.

    Start a new sketch on one of the small end faces of the current **Base Flange**, then use a **Corner Rectangle** to draw a second **Base Flange** sketch that is linked to the corners of the first **Base Flange** and is also 100mm wide, as illustrated in *Figure 8.2*.

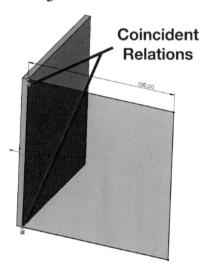

Figure 8.2: Sketching the second Base Flange, making it Coincident with the corners of the first one

3. Use the second sketch to create a **Base Flange** by selecting the **Base Flange/Tab** option and accepting the default parameters (the sheet thickness should still be 4mm).

Note that the `Cut list` folder in the FeatureManager Design Tree now has the number 2 in brackets next to it (see *Figure 8.3*). This indicates that we have two sheets within our model. The folder can be expanded, and the sheets can be hidden or shown by left-clicking on them and selecting **Hide** or **Show**:

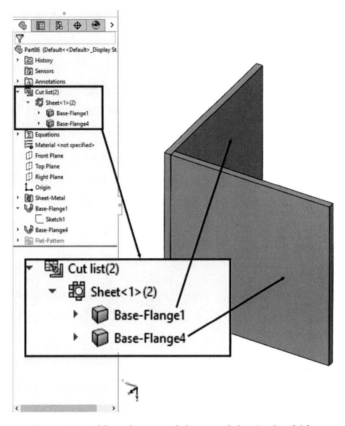

Figure 8.3: Adding the second sheet, and the Cut list folder

4. Now that we have the second sheet, we can start to create a **Tab and Slot** feature. Select **Tab and Slot** from the Sheet Metal tools. As with many SolidWorks tools, the options in the **Property Manager** initially look very complicated but there is a logical flow to them, and the message in the yellow box at the top of the **Property Manager** explains the process.

5. First, we need to select where the feature will be placed, using the boxes in the **Selection** section. The uppermost edge is the **Tab Edge** (labeled **i** in *Figure 8.4*) selection box. This is a linear edge where the tab will be placed:

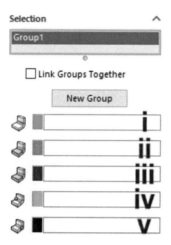

Figure 8.4: The Selection options

When working with sheets that join at a corner, as our example, it can be easier to select the *internal corner* instead of the *external corner*. This is because there is only one single edge here, whereas the outside corner has two edges (one from each sheet), so it can be difficult to select the correct edge.

Rotate the model and select the inside corner, as illustrated in *Figure 8.5*. Note that the start and end points of the selected edge are automatically added as green and purple points in the Graphics Area and added to corresponding selection boxes (labeled **iv** and **v** *Figure 8.4*).

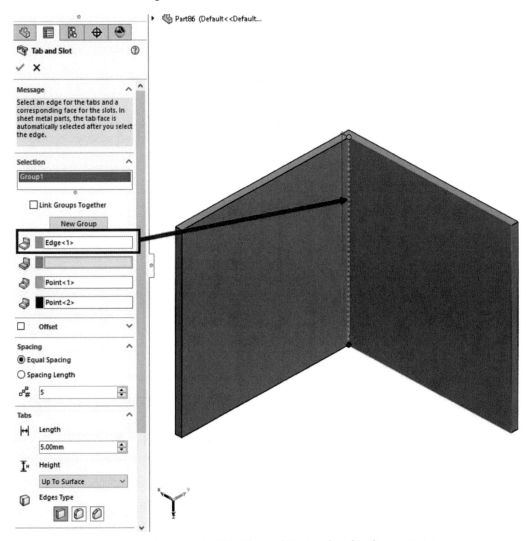

Figure 8.5: Selecting the Tab Edge and Start and End Reference Points

6. Next, we need to select the **Slot Face**.

Spin the model around and select the outside face, as shown in *Figure 8.6*. A yellow preview of the tabs and slots should now appear on the model:

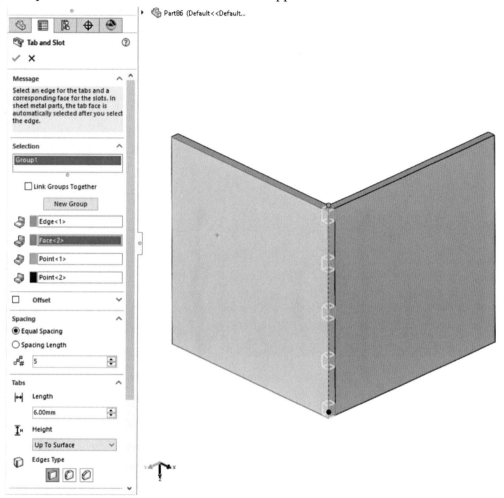

Figure 8.6: Selecting the Slot Face

7. Press the green **OK** check mark to create a **Tab and Slot** feature using the default sizes and options (see *Figure 8.7*). Note how one sheet has had the slots cut away and the other sheet has had the corresponding tabs added.

Two features now appear in the FeatureManager Design Tree—the **Tab and Slot-Tab** feature and the **Tab and Slot-Slot** feature. These two features are always added as a pair; you can't have one without the other. However, because they are on different sheets, they will appear as two different features.

Try expanding the Cut list folder and hiding each sheet in turn, to take a closer look at how they fit together. You can also hide sheets by hovering over them in the Graphics Area and pressing the **Tab** key (reshow them by pressing *Ctrl + Z* to undo, or by expanding the Cut list folder and pressing **Show** on the hidden sheet):

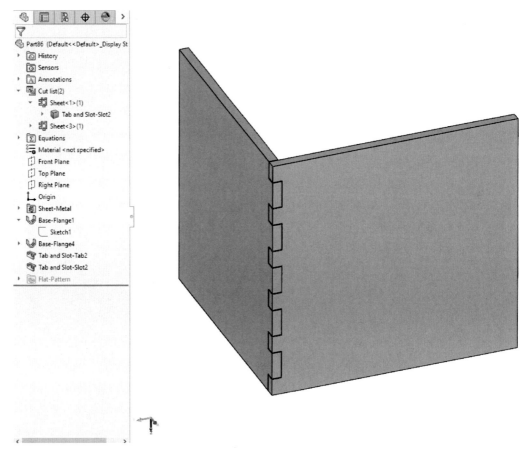

Figure 8.7: The created Tab and Slot features

We have now added a basic **Tab and Slot** feature and, hopefully, you can see how this would help with the joining of the two sheets. In the next section, we will look at editing the feature in order to set the properties that we want.

Adjusting Tab and Slot properties

In the previous section, we added the **Tab and Slot** features using the default options. However, there are many properties that can set the exact size and spacing of tabs and slots.

When editing the **Tab or Slot** feature, we have to edit the **Tab and Slot-Tab** feature in the FeatureManager Design Tree (see *Figure 8.8*). This will allow us to change both the tab and the slot details; it is not possible to edit the **Tab and Slot-Slot** feature directly:

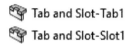

Figure 8.8: The Tab and Slot-Tab and Tab and Slot-Slot features

1. Edit the **Tab and Slot-Tab** feature by clicking on it in the FeatureManager Design Tree and pressing **Edit Feature**.

2. We can now specify the exact details of the tabs and slots. Firstly, we can specify where the tabs and slots will begin by setting an **Offset** if this is required.

    Select the **Offset** box and set both offsets to 10mm. These distances are measured from the **Start Reference Point** and **End Reference Point** (the green and purple *points* in the Graphics Area, as indicated in *Figure 8.9)*.

    Try adjusting the offsets and see how this changes the preview in the Graphics Area. Notice how the spacing between the slots decreases automatically as we increase the offsets:

Figure 8.9: The Start and End Reference Points

3. Next, we can set the **Spacing** values of the tabs and slots. It's possible to *either* set an **Equal Spacing** value and specify how many tabs will be added *or* to set a **Spacing Length** value, meaning that the number of tabs will be automatically adjusted to fit within that length.

   Depending on the values used, both of these options can give very similar results, and the choice of which to use is largely down to personal preference.

   Set an **Equal Spacing** value with six instances.

4. The **Tab** details can be changed next.

   The **Length** value is simply a numerical value. Set this to 5mm.

   The **Height** value can be set using three end conditions, as follows:

   - **Up To Surface**: The tabs will reach all the way through the sheet where the slots are cut.

   - **Blind**: A simple numerical value can be set.

   - **Offset From Surface**: This can be used if the tabs need to either be shorter or extend beyond the sheet, and it can be useful for extending tabs in order to give more weld material.

   The **Edges Type** selection allows the corners of the tabs to either be **Sharp Edge**, **Fillet Edge**, or **Chamfer Edge**.

5. Finally, the **Slot** details can be set.

   The first option is **No Through Cut**. By default, the slots will go all the way through the face that they are made on. By selecting this option, we can create a partial slot cut that doesn't go all the way through the face.

> **Slot Depth Is Linked to Tab Height**
>
> If you deselect **No Through Cut** to make a partial slot cut, then be aware that the depths of the slots are linked to the height of the tabs. Therefore, if your tab height is still set to the **Up To Surface** option, then selecting **No Through Cut** for the slots won't actually change the slot depth. To do this, you will also have to reduce the tab height.
>
> Also, be aware that creating partial slot cuts in sheet metal, in real life, is much more difficult than simply creating through cuts, and as such, this might increase the cost and lead time of your parts.

6. Next, we can set the **Offset** amount of the slots, as illustrated in *Figure 8.10*. This is how much larger the slots will be compared to the tabs. Slots always have to be slightly larger so that tabs can fit into them, and so it's not possible to set the **Offset** amount to zero, although a very small number can be set instead.

    Selecting **Equal offset** will make both the **Length** and the **Width** values of the offsets have the same value.

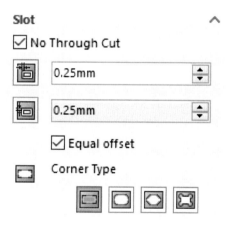

Figure 8.10: Slot options

7. The very last option in the **Slot** section allows the **Corner Type** field to be set, with **Sharp**, **Filleted**, **Chamfered**, and **Circular** options available.

Corner-Type Limitations

If you encounter an error when trying to use **Filleted** or **Chamfered** corner types, then try reducing the size of the **Filleted** or **Chamfered** corner or increasing the **Offset** value, or both.

Sometimes, the size of the fillet or chamfer in the corners can effectively reduce the actual distance and, in some cases, completely remove any gap, causing an error when trying to create the feature, as illustrated in *Figure 8.11*.

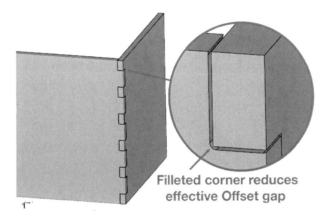

Filleted corner reduces
effective Offset gap

Figure 8.11: Be aware that filleted or chamfered corners may need a bigger offset gap

The **Tab and Slot** tool has many options that allow you exactly set the size, spacing, and type of feature that you want.

Summary

In this chapter, we learned that the **Tab and Slot** tool is a great way of joining two sheets together, especially if they meet at a perpendicular angle. Slots will be cut from one of the sheets, and the adjoining sheets will have tabs added that fit into these slots.

In the next chapter, we will take a close look at the various **Corner** tools that allow you to easily finish off the small details of your models.

9
Finishing Off Models Using Corner Details

SolidWorks Sheet Metal contains a number of **Corner tools** that can be used for many different operations, including closing corner gaps between flanges, adding welded corners, trimming away sharp edges, and adding corner relief around bend areas.

By the end of this chapter, you'll understand how to use the four different **Corner** tools.

In this chapter, we're going to cover the following main topics:

- Reducing gaps by using **Closed Corners**
- Removing corners gaps by adding **Welded Corners**
- Getting rid of sharp corners with the **Break-Corner/Corner-Trim** tool
- Preparing your model for manufacturing using **Corner Relief**

Reducing gaps by using Closed Corners

The **Corner** tools are a set of four similar tools that are grouped together because they all deal with corner details. Individually, the tools are fairly simple but they can be useful for saving time or creating a specific feature in your models.

The first tool is the **Closed Corner**. This can be used to reduce the gaps that can occur between two adjacent flanges.

To show an example of the **Closed Corner** tool, first we will create a simple part with some adjacent flanges:

1. Start a new *part* document and use the **Center Rectangle** tool to create a **Base Flange** that is fixed to the **Origin** and is 50x50mm in size and 2mm thick. The default **Sheet Metal** properties can be used.

2. Add two **Edge Flanges** to any of the adjacent edges (*Figure 9.1*). Make these 30mm high and at a 90° angle.

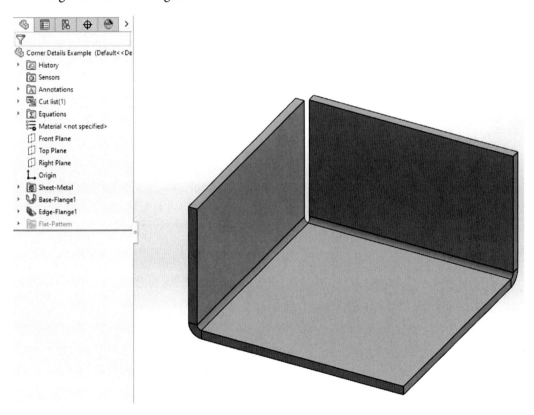

Figure 9.1: Creating a Base Flange with two adjacent Edge Flanges

3. Spin the model around and note that we currently have a gap in the corner, between the two **Edge Flanges**. Select the **Closed Corner** tool from the drop-down menu underneath the **Corners** button in the **Sheet Metal** tools.

4. First, we need to select where we want to close the gap. Ensure that you have the top selection box – **Faces to Extend** – active and then select the end face of either of the **Edge Flanges** (*Figure 9.2*):

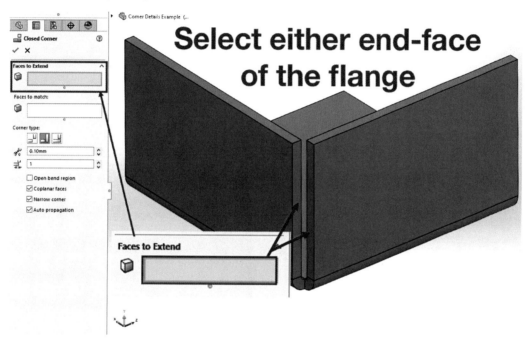

Figure 9.2: Selecting the Faces to Extend

5. A preview will now appear showing that the selected face has been extended and the corresponding face has been extended a smaller amount to reduce the corner gap (*Figure 9.3*). Note that the second face has automatically been selected as the **Face to match**. It is also possible to manually select the **Faces to match** if needed.

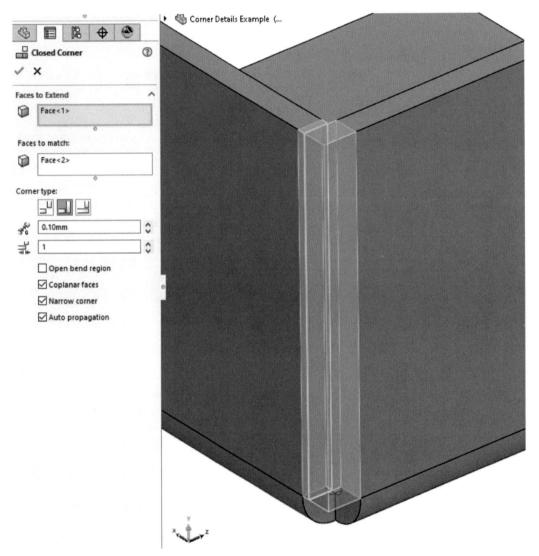

Figure 9.3: The Face to Extend is extended and the Face to match is extended by a smaller amount

6. We can now select the **Corner Type**. Try selecting each type in turn, to see the differences, by clicking each of the three buttons:

    - **Butt**: This extends each face slightly, so that the gap is reduced but the flanges don't overlap each other (*Figure 9.4*, left). The **Gap distance** can be set using a numerical value.

    - **Overlap**: This extends one of the flanges so that it overlaps the corresponding one (*Figure 9.4*, center). For this option, we can set the **Gap distance** and also the **Overlap/underlap ratio**. This controls how much the longer flange overlaps the shorter one. A value of 1 will mean the overlap covers the whole of the flange, whereas a value of 0.5 (for example) means that the overlap will cover half of the flange.

    - **Underlap**: This is very similar to the **Overlap** option but the flanges are reversed (*Figure 9.4*, right):

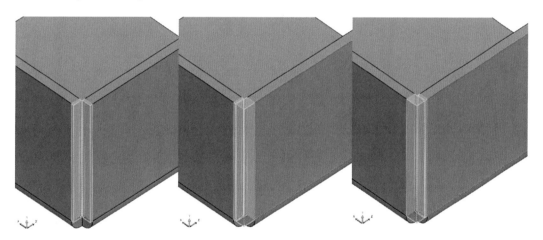

Figure 9.4: Corner Type options; from left to right: Butt, Overlap, Underlap

Set the **Corner Type** to **Overlap**.

7. Ensure that the **Open bend region** option is checked. This will automatically trim away a corner relief area when filling the gap. It is possible to create Closed Corners without this option selected (*Figure 9.5*) but it can result in manufacturing complications and can sometimes cause model errors if the **Gap distance** is too small.

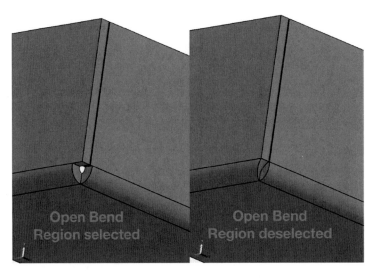

Figure 9.5: Closed Corner with Open bend region selected (left) and deselected (right)

8. Press the green **OK** check mark to create the **Closed Corner**. Note that although we do still have a small gap (due to the nature of sheet metal, with folded flanges) it is much reduced.

9. There are also three other options that can be used with the **Closed Corner** tool. These can be seen by editing the **Closed Corner** feature:

    • **Coplanar faces**: Selecting this option will mean that **Closed Corner** will be applied to all faces that are *coplanar* (lined up) with the selected faces, even if those coplanar faces are not selected themselves. This can be useful if one of the flanges has a cut in it that breaks the surface up into smaller sections (*Figure 9.6*):

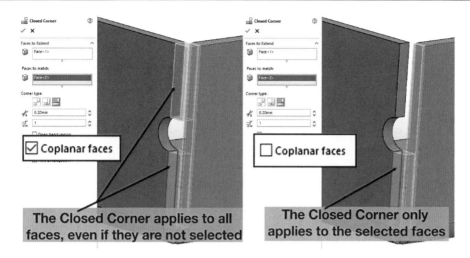

Figure 9.6: Selecting Coplanar faces will apply the Closed Corner to all coplanar faces,
even if only one is selected

- **Narrow Corner**: This can reduce the gap distance around the bend area,
  depending on your model's exact geometry. However, it usually only makes
  a small difference.

- **Auto propagation**: This option simply automatically selects the corresponding
  Faces to match when the **Faces to Extend** are selected.

The **Closed Corner** can be especially useful when working with flanges that are not at 90°
to the **Base Flange** (*Figure 9.7*). In these cases, the gap distance will vary along the length
of the flange, and so using the **Closed Corner** tool allows these gaps to easily be closed.

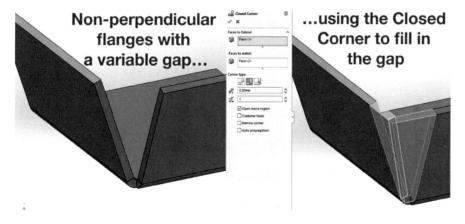

Figure 9.7: Using the Closed Corner tool to close gaps between non-perpendicular/parallel flanges

The **Closed Corner** tool is a great way of reducing the gaps between adjacent flanges but sometimes you might want to remove the gaps entirely. In the next section, we will look at how you can use the **Welded Corners** tool to do this.

Removing corner gaps by adding Welded Corners

The **Welded Corners** tool can completely close a corner gap by welding the corners together. This tool is the simplest of the four **Corner Tools** and can be used as follows:

1. Delete the **Closed Corner** feature from the previous section so that we just have a single **Base Flange** (50x50x2mm) with two adjacent **Edge Flanges** that are 30mm high and at a 90° angle.

2. Select the **Welded Corner** tool from the **Sheet Metal Corner** tools.

3. Now we simply need to select the side face of one of the **Edge Flanges**.

   We will then see a yellow preview of the **Welded Corner** (*Figure 9.8*):

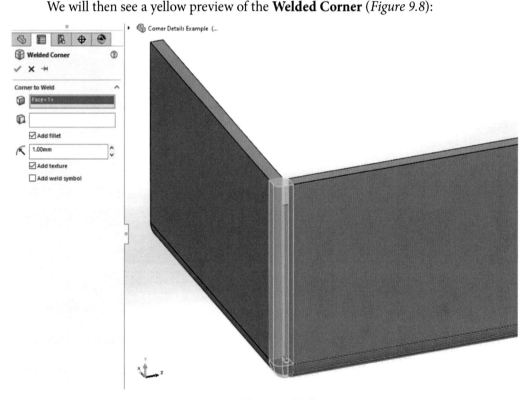

Figure 9.8: Adding a Welded Corner

4. By default, the **Welded Corner** will run the full length of the selected face, but if needed, a stopping point can be added by creating a sketch with a *point* in it, on the side face of the flange, *before* creating the **Welded Corner**.

5. A welded area can be rounded off by selecting the **Add fillet** option. There are also options to **Add texture** to the welded area and to **Add weld symbol**.

6. Press the green **OK** check mark to create the feature. The welded material will count towards the model's *mass* and *volume* that can be displayed using the **Mass Properties** tool on the **Evaluate** tab. The **Mass Properties** tool also contains an option to specifically **Show weld bead mass**.

7. Note that when the model is **Flattened**, the **Welded Corners** will automatically be suppressed to allow the sheet to unfold correctly.

The **Welded Corner** tool is a very simple feature that can be used to join adjacent edges. In the next section, we will look at how the **Break-Corner/Corner-Trim** tool can be used to remove sharp edges.

Getting rid of sharp corners with the Break-Corner/Corner-Trim tool

The **Break-Corner/Corner-Trim** tool is very similar to **Fillet** and **Chamfer** tools in that it allows square corners to be easily removed by filleting or chamfering them. This can be used to make items easier to manufacture, can be for structural reasons, or can even just make parts more user-friendly by taking off sharp corners.

To use the **Break-Corner/Corner-Trim** tool, perform the following steps:

1. Continuing from the previous example, delete the **Welded Corner** feature so that you just have a single **Base Flange** (50x50x2mm) with two adjacent **Edge Flanges** that are 30mm high and at a 90° angle.

2. Select the **Break-Corner/Corner-Trim** tool from the **Corner** tools.

3. First, we can set a **Break Type** – either **Filleted** or **Chamfered** – and then set the **Size**.

   Chose **Fillet** and set the size to 5mm.

4. We can now select the corners that we wish to break. The corners can be left-clicked directly, or the entire face can be selected and all relevant corners will be broken. In this way, the **Break-Corner/Corner-Trim** tool is much more useful than the Fillet or Chamfer tools, because we don't have to zoom in a lot to select the very short edges of the flanges; we can simply select the entire face.

Select both of the **Edge Flanges**, and the **Base Flange**, as shown in *Figure 9.9*:

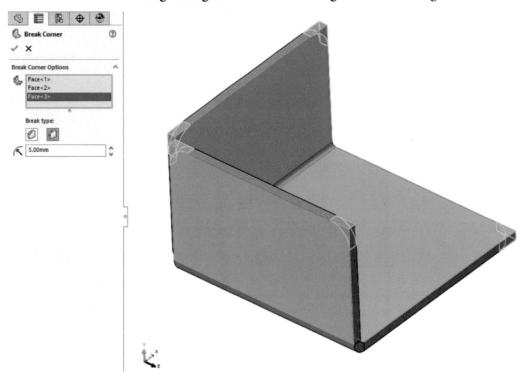

Figure 9.9: Adding the Break Corner feature

5. Press the green **OK** check mark to add the **Break-Corner/Corner-Trim** feature.

So far, we have just created *external* broken corners, but the tool can also be used with *internal* corners, as shown in the next section.

Using the Break-Corner/Corner-Trim tool with internal corners

Follow these steps to use this tool with internal corners:

1. Add a **Tab** to the **Base Flange**, by sketching a rectangle on the upper face, then selecting the **Base Flange/Tab** tool (*Figure 9.10*):

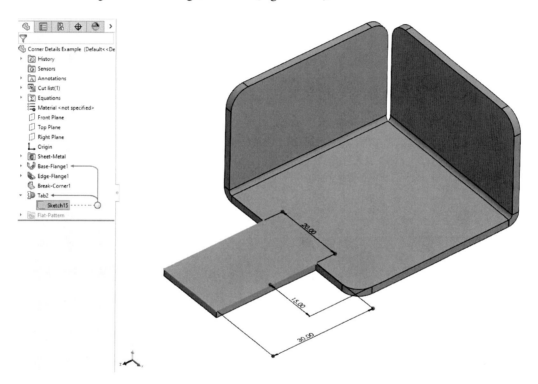

Figure 9.10: Adding a Tab to the Base Flange

2. Select the **Break-Corner/Corner-Trim** tool again.

3. Using the same settings as before (**Fillet**, 5mm size), select the **Base Flange** face again. Note how just the *external* corners are selected (*Figure 9.11*):

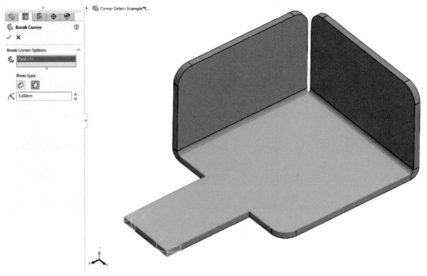

Figure 9.11: Selecting the Base Flange face

4. Zoom in and manually select the two *internal* corners (*Figure 9.12*). Creating internal broken corners adds material, whereas creating external broken corners removes material.

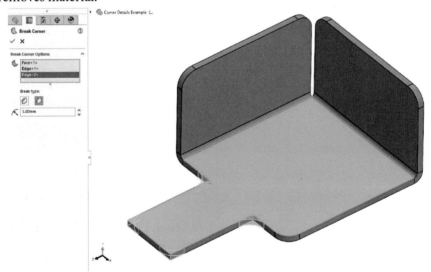

Figure 9.12: Manually selecting internal corners

5. Press the green **OK** check mark to add the new broken corners.

As well as using the **Break-Corner/Corner-Trim** tool on folded parts, it can also be used on flattened models to quickly select all corners together.

Using the Break-Corner/Corner-Trim tool on flattened models

There may be many cases where you create an entire Sheet Metal model without adding any trimmed corners but wish to add them all at the end of your modeling, perhaps to aid with manufacturing.

In these cases, the **Break-Corner/Corner-Trim** tool can be used after flattening the part:

1. Continuing from the previous example, delete any current **Break-Corner/ Corner-Trim** features so that you just have the **Base Flange**, **Tab**, and two **Edge Flange** features.

2. Flatten the model by clicking the **Flatten** button.

3. Now expand the drop-down menu for the **Corner** tools and you'll see that only one option is available, **Corner-Trim**. This is very similar to the previous tool that we used in the last section but specialized for flattened models. Select the **Corner-Trim** tool (*Figure 9.13*):

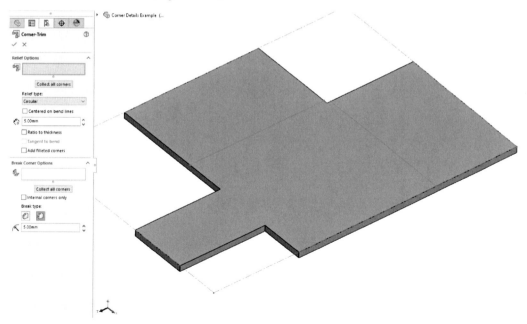

Figure 9.13: Using the Corner-Trim tool with a flattened part

4. We now have the ability to add **Relief Options** and to add **Break Corner Options**. We will cover the **Relief Options** in the next section and just look at the **Break Corner Options** for now.

   As before, we can set the **Break type** and **Size**.

   Set **Filleted**, 5mm size.

5. Next, select the corners to be broken. When using this tool in the flattened state, we have two new options. Clicking the **Collect all corners** button will automatically select all relevant corners in the model. We can also check the **Internal corners only** box to just select internal corners (external corners have to be selected manually).

   Click **Collect all corners** to select the bends in the model.

   > Using the Collect all corners Button versus Selecting the Face
   >
   > When selecting the corners to break, I recommend using the **Collect all corners** button, instead of just selecting the face. This is because sometimes selecting the face will also mistakenly select corners within bends, which shouldn't be broken.

6. Press the green **OK** check mark to break the selected corners. Note that the **Corner-Trim** feature now appears after the **Flat-Pattern** folder in the FeatureManager Design Tree.

7. Unflatten the part by selecting the **Flatten** button again. Note that the trimmed corners no longer appear in the model and the **Corner-Trim** feature is suppressed (turned off). This is because the **Corner-Trim** feature is a *child feature* of the **Flat-Pattern** feature. Therefore, if the **Flat-Pattern** feature is suppressed (such as when the model is unflattened) then the **Corner-Trim** feature is also suppressed.

Using the **Corner-Trim** tool after flattening in this way is an example of one of the few times where you might add features to the model after the **Flat-Pattern** folder at the end of your modeling.

If you require the corners to be trimmed in the unflattened state, then you can use the **Corner/Corner-Trim** tool as described earlier in this chapter, or you can use the **Unfold** feature to flatten your part, then manually trim all of the corners, then use the **Fold** feature to fold the part back up.

In the next section, we will take a look at the final corner tool, **Corner Relief**.

Preparing your model for manufacturing using Corner Relief

The **Corner Relief** tool allows us to add relief cuts to the corners in our model. This can be useful for avoiding manufacturing issues in tight corners where two or more bends meet.

The tool can be used in the unflattened or flattened state and we will look at the unflattened version first:

1. Continuing from the previous example, delete any current **Break-Corner/Corner-Trim** features so that you just have the **Base Flange**, **Tab**, and two **Edge Flange** features. Ensure that the model is in the Unflattened (that is, folded-up) state.

2. Select the **Corner Relief** tool from the drop-down menu underneath the **Corner** tools. We can now set some options in the Property Manager (*Figure 9.14*):

Figure 9.14: Corner Relief Property Manager

3. The **Scope** section simply indicates which sheet we are working with. This is usually automatically prefilled but if working in a multi-sheet part, then you can select the appropriate sheet.

4. Next, we need to select either a **2 Bend Corner** or a **3 Bend Corner**. In our current model, we only have a 2 Bend Corner. This means that the corner has two bends that are next to each other (*Figure 9.15*). In the next section, we will look at 3 Bend Corners.

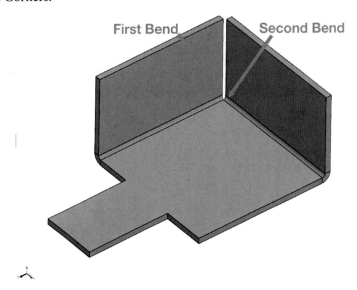

Figure 9.15: A 2 Bend Corner

Select **2 Bend Corner** then click the **Collect all corners** button in the **Corners** section.

Notice how the **Define Corner** box has now been filled with the two faces from the bend.

5. We can now set the **Relief Options**. There are five main options, each of which produces a slightly different style of cut. Each version also has a number of sub-options:

- **Rectangular**: This will cut out a rectangular area. The cut size can either be determined by a numerical value in the **Slot length** box or by checking the **Ratio to thickness** box, which calculates the size according to the sheet thickness.

   The **Centered on bend lines** option centers the cut relative to the bend lines, and the **Tangent to bend** option makes the cut tangent to the bend lines (*Figure 9.16*).

   The **Add filleted corners** button simply rounds off the sharp corners of the relief cut.

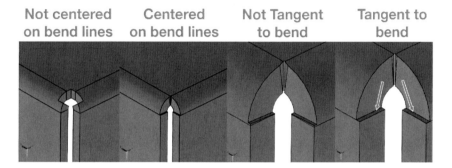

Figure 9.16: The Centered on bend and Tangent to bend options

- **Circular**: Produces a circular cut out.
- **Tear**: Creates a torn relief; there are no sub-options available.
- **Obround**: This creates an obround (slot-shaped) cut.
- **Constant Width**: This makes a linear and continuous cut with a constant width and it has no sub-options.

   Experiment with the different types of **Corner Relief** cut to see the differences between them on the preview in the Graphics Area.

6. Press the green **OK** check mark to create the **Corner Relief** cuts.

As well as *2 Bend Corners*, the **Corner Relief** tool can also be used with more unusual *3 Bend Corners*.

Using the Corner Relief option with 3 Bend Corners

3 Bend Corners tend to be a little less common in Sheet Metal models but we will briefly take a look at one now:

1. Continuing with the previous model, add two further **Edge Flanges** as shown in *Figure 9.17*. This will create a 3 Bend Corner (we have just added two more bends, and we previously had one bend from the first set of **Edge Flanges**).

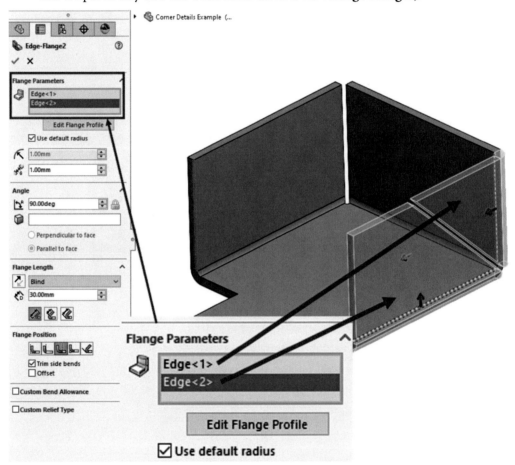

Figure 9.17: Adding a 3 Bend Corner

2. We can now use the same corner tool so select the **Corner Relief** tool from the **Corners** drop-down menu.

3. Under the **Corner Type** section, select **3 Bend Corner**.

4. Press the **Collect all corners** button and note that the 3 Bend Corner is selected, and all three of the faces are added to the **Define Corner** section.

5. We can now use the **Relief Options** section to add the corner relief cuts in the same way as for 2 Bend Corners.

In this manner, we can use multiple **Corner Relief** features to add relief cuts for different corner types when the model is in the folded state, but we can also use the **Corner Relief** tool with flattened parts.

Adding Corner Relief cuts to flattened models

Sometimes you may wish to complete the majority of your Sheet Metal model first, then add relief cuts to the entire design at the end of modeling. When using this method, it can be easier to apply the cuts to the flattened model:

1. After the majority of your modeling is complete, flatten the model by pressing the **Flatten** button.

2. Click the drop-down menu underneath the **Corner** tools. Select the **Corner-Trim** option – the only one that is available in the flattened state. This is the same tool that we used in the previous section to break the sharp corners, but it can also be used to add corner relief.

3. Click the **Collect all corners** button under the **Relief Options** section. Note that in the flattened state, we don't need to specify 2 or 3 Bend Corners – they are both treated the same.

4. Set the **Relief Type** and **Size**. This can either be **Circular**, **Square**, or **Bend Waist** (*Figure 9.18*):

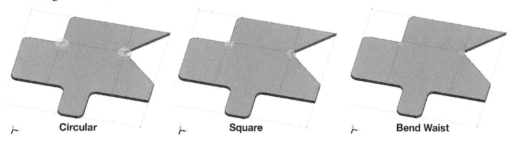

Figure 9.18: Relief cut types

5. Press the green **OK** check mark to add the relief cuts. Note that these reliefs will only appear in the flattened state. If the model is unflattened, then the **Corner Relief** feature will be suppressed.

In this way, relief cuts can easily all be added together at the same time.

Summary

In this chapter, we looked at the four **Corner** tools. The first one, **Closed Corner**, allows us to reduce corner gaps between adjacent flanges, whereas the **Welded Corner** tool lets us completely remove these gaps. The **Break-Corner/Corner-Trim** tool speeds up the removal of sharp edges, and the final tool, **Corner Relief**, adds relief cuts that may be required for manufacturing reasons.

In the next chapter, we will explore how we can add 3D detail to our flat sheets by creating and using **Forming Tools**.

10
Adding 3D Details to Models with Forming Tools

So far, we have learned how to add **three-dimensional** (**3D**) details to flat sheets by using features such as **Edge Flanges**. However, it is also possible to add 3D features by using **Forming Tools**. These are specially made tools that are commonly used to press shapes into flat faces.

This chapter explains how to use existing Forming Tools from the SolidWorks **Design Library**, as well as how to modify Forming Tools and create and use entirely Custom Forming Tools.

In this chapter, we're going to cover the following main topics:

- Using Forming Tools
- Modifying existing Forming Tools
- Creating Custom Forming Tools

Using Forming Tools

Forming Tools are shaped tools, known as dies, that are pressed into flat sheets under high pressure, leaving an indentation behind. Some Forming Tools can even create cuts within the sheet, as well as shaped impressions. Examples of these shapes include things such as dimples, louvers (shaped vents), and even logos and text. You can see some examples of shapes created using forming tools in *Figure 10.1*:

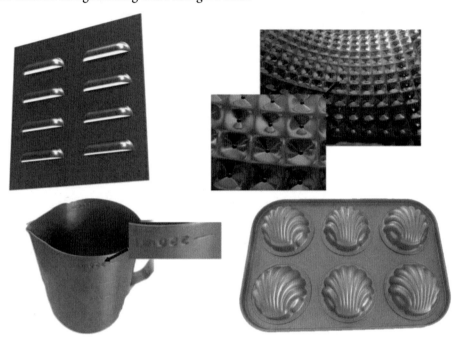

Figure 10.1: Examples of shapes created using forming tools

The SolidWorks **Design Library** includes many premade Forming Tools that can easily be used when working with Sheet Metal models. Because these tools are available in a fairly limited range of shapes and sizes, they may not be that useful for your needs, but they can be modified; the later sections in this chapter will show how to do this, as well as how to create entirely Custom Forming Tools.

To demonstrate the use of Forming Tools first we will make a simple Sheet Metal part, as follows:

1. Start a new *part* document and use the **Center Rectangle** tool to create a **Base Flange** that is fixed to the Origin and is 50x50mm in size and 1mm thick. The default Sheet Metal properties can be used.

2. Open the **Design Library** by clicking on the icon (it looks like a set of books) in the **Task Pane** at the right-hand side of the screen, as indicated in *Figure 10.2*.

    If you do not see the **Task Pane**, then it can be switched on by right-clicking on the **Command Manager** and ensuring that there is a check mark next to **Tools | Task Pane**.

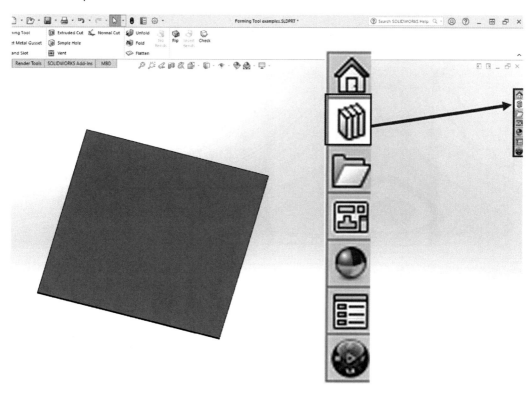

Figure 10.2: Opening the Design Library tab

3. Expand the `Design Library` folder within the **Task Pane** and expand the `Forming Tools` folder. You should now see a number of different Forming Tool types, such as **embosses** and **ribs**. Click on `embosses` and note that the various embossing tools available will be shown at the bottom of the **Task Pane**. **Note**: Depending on your settings and SolidWorks version, your **Design Library** may appear slightly different from how it looks in *Figure 10.3*.

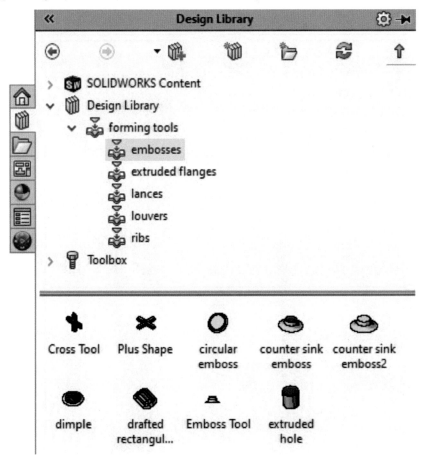

Figure 10.3: Expanding the Design Library and the Forming Tools folder

> **If the Design Library Is Not Visible**
>
> If you can't see the **Design Library** within the **Task Pane**, then you need to relink SolidWorks to the correct folder.
>
> This can be done by going to **Tools | Options | System Options | File Locations**.
>
> Then, find **Design Library** in the drop-down list and ensure that the location of your `Design Library` folder appears within the **Folders** box. If the folder is not there, click **Add** and find the location of your **Design Library** on your computer's hard drive.
>
> By default, this location is usually `C:\ProgramData\SolidWorks\ SolidWorks 20xx\Design Library`.
>
> (Note that the `Program Data` folder is often a hidden folder, so you may need to adjust your **Windows Explorer** view settings to show hidden folders.)
>
> Then, press **OK** to add the `Design Library` folder, and it should now appear within the **Task Pane**.

To use the Forming Tools, they can simply be dragged into the model by holding the left mouse button and dragging the desired tool onto the sheet face.

4. As an example, select the `embosses` subfolder within the `forming tools` folder in the **Task Pane**, then left-click and drag the **counter sink emboss** tool onto the top face of your **Base Flange**.

   A yellow preview of the indentation that will be made should now appear on your model in the **Graphics Area**, as illustrated in *Figure 10.4*:

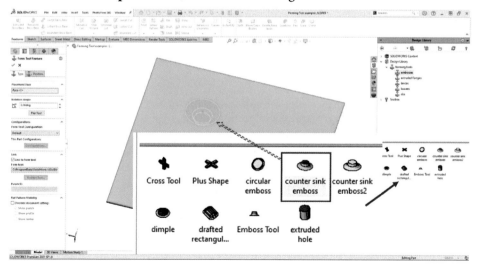

Figure 10.4: Dragging the Forming Tool onto the model

Are You Trying to Make a Derived Part?

If you try to drag the tool onto the sheet and are presented with the message, **Are you trying to make a Derived Part?**, this simply means that SolidWorks does not recognize that you are working with Forming Tools. To fix this, close the error message box by selecting **Cancel**. Then, open the **Task Pane** again, right-click on the `forming tools` folder, and place a check mark next to the **Forming Tools Folder** option. This will ensure that SolidWorks knows that all *parts* within the folder should be treated as Forming Tool *parts*.

5. Press the green **OK** check mark to insert the **counter sink emboss** feature. We should now see that the sheet has been deformed in the shape of the tool that we selected, and there is a hole in the center of the embossed area, as illustrated in *Figure 10.5*. If we look at the various Forming Tools in the **Design Library** (*Figure 10.4—lower right*), we can see that they are colored yellow or red. A yellow face indicates that the face of the tool will deform (or bend) the sheet, whereas a red face indicates material that will be cut away (for more information on this, see the *Creating Custom Forming Tools* section, later in this chapter):

Figure 10.5: The Forming Tool feature

We can edit the **Forming Tool** feature in the usual way, or we can expand the feature and edit the position sketch underneath the feature if we simply want to change the position of the feature.

6. Left-click on the **counter sink emboss** feature in the FeatureManager Design Tree and select **Edit Feature**.

The **Forming Tool** feature is similar to the **Hole Wizard** in that it contains a **Type** tab that can be used to adjust the actual tool details, and it also contains a **Position** tab that allows one or more instances to be positioned.

The **Type** tab (*Figure 10.6*) provides the following options:

- **Placement Face**: This sets the face where the tool will be pressed into.

- **Rotation Angle**: The tool can be rotated to any angle here. It can also be flipped, allowing the tool to be pressed in from the opposite side of the sheet.

- **Configurations**: The Forming Tools are *part* files in their own right (more details on this in the next two sections in this chapter) and therefore can have multiple configurations. This section allows you to set the required configuration if needed.

- **Link**: This section allows you to keep or break the link to the Forming Tool *part*. If the link is kept and the Forming Tool *part* is subsequently changed, then the feature in this model will also change.

- **Flat Pattern Visibility**: By default, the **Forming Tool** features will not appear in Flat Patterns; however, this can be overridden by selecting this checkbox.

Figure 10.6: The Forming Tool Type tab

7. The **Position** tab can now be used to place the tool features. Select the **Position** tab and the cursor will change to the **Point** tool.

    Similar to the **Hole Wizard**, a Forming Feature will be placed anywhere that a *point* is placed.

    The **Smart Dimension** tool can also be used to set the exact position of the features.

8. Once you are happy with the position and type of the features, press the green **OK** check mark to create them.

The basic Forming Tools in the SolidWorks **Design Library** can be useful, but the selection is quite limited; therefore, it's likely that you will need to modify these tools to suit your own needs. In the next section, we will look at how to do this.

Modifying existing Forming Tools

The SolidWorks **Toolbox** and **Hole Wizard** features both contain many size variations and so are extremely useful. By contrast, the Forming Tools available in the SolidWorks **Design Library** only come in a very limited range of sizes. However, although the *size range* of these tools is limited, there are quite a few different *types* of tools. Therefore, it's likely that you can find a similar shape or type of Forming Tool to address your needs, then modify the size so that it exactly suits your requirements.

To modify Forming Tools:

1. Start a new *part* document and use the **Center Rectangle** tool to create a **Base Flange** that is fixed to the Origin and is 50x50mm in size and 1mm thick. The default Sheet Metal properties can be used.

    You can also use the model from the previous section and simply delete the Forming Tool features.

2. The first step in modifying Forming Tools is to find a similar tool to your requirements. For example, if you want an extruded flange with a cutout, expand the **extruded flanges** section and find the **rectangular flange** tool, as shown in *Figure 10.7*. Remember that yellow faces in the tool will bend the sheet metal and red faces will cut away material:

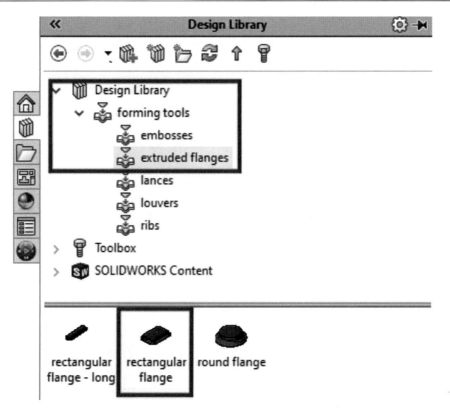

Figure 10.7: Finding an existing tool that is similar to your requirements

3. Next, we need to open the tool in order to modify it. Right-click on the preview of the **rectangular flange** tool (in the **Task Pane**—see *Figure 10.7*) and select **Open**. We will now be taken to the *part* document for the tool. (**Note**: You may receive a Write Access warning. This can be ignored as we will not be saving over the original *part* file.) The *part* can be edited in the same way as a normal model—for example, the extrude features can be adjusted in size by editing their underlying sketches or by left-clicking on the appropriate feature in the Graphics Area, then double-clicking any dimension and changing it.

4. Adjust the size of the main rectangular area (the `Boss-Extrude1` feature) by changing the dimensions from `30x20mm` to `50x30mm`, as illustrated in *Figure 10.8*.

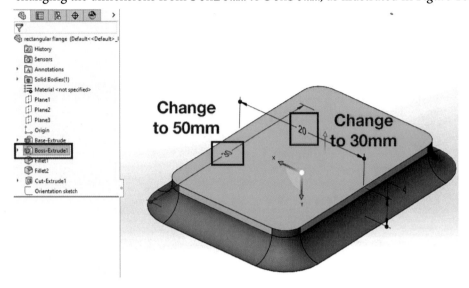

Figure 10.8: Adjusting the Forming Tool size

5. Note that the Fillet that was running around the base of the tool no longer travels all the way around the tool (*Figure 10.9*). This Fillet is important for ensuring that the tool works correctly (sharp edges on Forming Tools can potentially cause manufacturing issues):

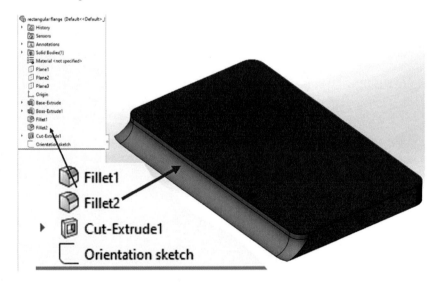

Figure 10.9: The Fillet around the bottom of the tool is no longer correct

Therefore, to ensure that this Fillet is created properly, extend the size of the Base-Extrude feature by the same amount as we extended the tool shape in *Step 4*.

6. So, edit the Base-Extrude feature or sketch and add 20mm to the long edge and 10mm to the short edge, as illustrated in *Figure 10.10*.

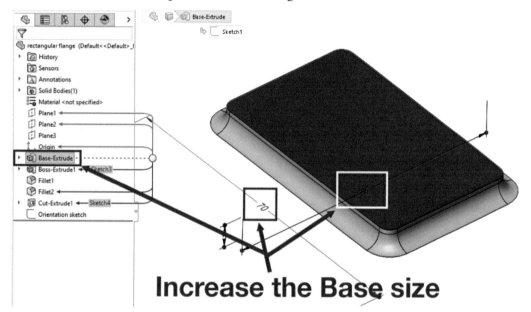

Figure 10.10: Increasing the base size

Notice that after increasing the base size, the Fillet now follows the lower outline correctly.

7. We can now save the *part* for use, as follows:

    I.   Select **File | Save As…**

    II. Select **Save as copy and open** from the lower left of the dialog box.

Save As Copy

By saving the file as a copy, we maintain the original Forming Tool part (the **rectangular flange** tool) and save the modified version as an entirely new part. This means that models that use the original Forming Tool will be unaffected by these latest changes.

III.   Note that the **Save as type** dialog is displaying `Form Tool (*.sldftp)`. This indicates that the document will be saved as a specific *Form Tool Part* document.

IV.   The save location should default to the `extruded flanges` subfolder in the `forming tools` folder (the same location as the original **rectangular flange** tool that we started with). By saving in this folder, the *Form Tool Part* will be recognized as a Forming Tool and will appear in the `forming tools` folders in the **Design Library**.

Select **Save as copy and open**, then save the modified Forming Tool with a new filename, such as `Larger Rectangular Flange`.

8.   Return to the original document (the **Base Flange** sheet) by selecting it from the **Window** menu or by pressing the *Ctrl + Tab* keys to switch between open documents.

9.   Expand the **Task Pane** and note that the new Forming Tool—**Larger Rectangular Flange**—now appears with the other Forming Tools, as illustrated in *Figure 10.11*. This tool can then be dragged into the model and used in the same way as any other Forming Tool:

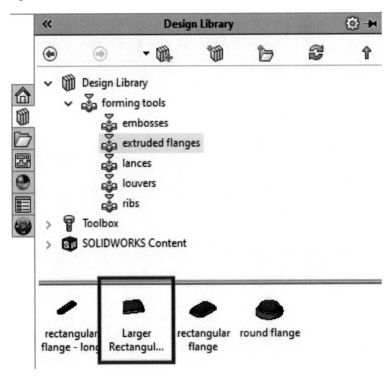

Figure 10.11: The saved Forming Tool now appears with the other tools

If the New Forming Tool Doesn't Appear

If the new *Form Tool Part* doesn't appear with the other Forming Tools in the **Design Library**, then it was probably saved in a different location from the other Forming Tools.

This can be fixed by opening the *Form Tool Part* (or press *Ctrl + Tab* to return to the document if you still have it open). Then, expand the **Task Pane** and select the **Add to Library** button at the top of the **Task Pane** (*Figure 10.12*). The part can then be added to the appropriate folder in the **Design Library** and used in the same way as the other Forming Tools.

Note: If you are using this method then the file needs to be saved before it is added to the **Design Library**.

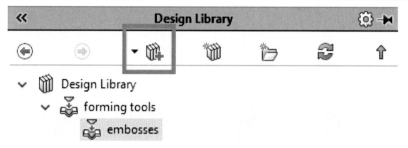

Figure 10.12: The Add to Library button

Although the standard Forming Tools in the **Design Library** are quite limited in variety they can be easily modified, allowing you to adjust them to suit your own needs. In the next section, we will look at taking this one step further by creating entirely **Custom Forming Tools**.

Creating Custom Forming Tools

Modifying existing Forming Tools may be suitable in many situations, but sometimes you might require an entirely custom tool. This could be something such as an unusually shaped indent or vent, a product's operating instructions or markings, or even your company logo. In these cases, we can create Custom Forming Tools. These tools are reasonably straightforward to make within SolidWorks, but be aware that creating and using Custom Forming Tools in real-life manufacturing is likely to add cost and lead time to your parts.

To make a Custom Forming Tool, we first create a shape as a normal *part* document, and then we convert it to a Forming Tool and save it as the appropriate file type, as follows:

1. Start a new *part* document and sketch a base on the **Top Plane**. This base is only used to help with tool setup and will be cut away from the model before use, so the exact size isn't critical, but it should always be larger than the main tool shape in both directions.

    In this case, sketch a **Center Rectangle** that is 50x50mm in size and fixed to the Origin. Then Extrude it 10mm, as illustrated in *Figure 10.13*.

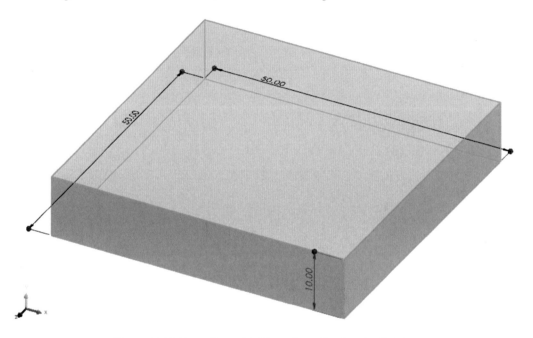

Figure 10.13: Extruding a 50x50mm base, fixed to the Origin

2. Next, we need to create a forming shape for the tool. That is the shape that will actually be pressed into the metal sheet when the tool is used.

3. Start a sketch on the upper face of the base extrude and use the **Polygon** tool to sketch a hexagon (six-sided polygon) that is 3 0mm in size across the flat edges. This should be centered on the Origin.

Extrude the hexagon 1 0mm upward, as illustrated in *Figure 10.14*.

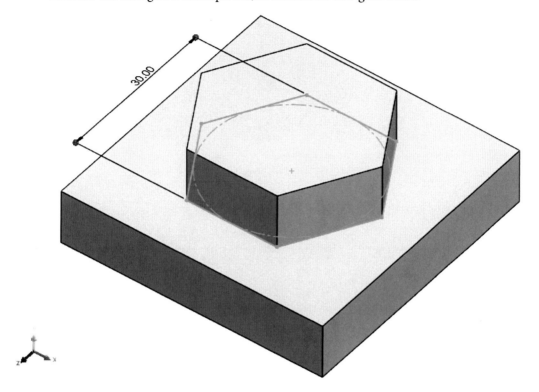

Figure 10.14: Extruding a 30mm hexagon, 10mm high

4. Generally, when making Forming Tools (and working with sheet metal), it is desirable to avoid sharp edges. With Forming Tools in particular, sharp edges can cause manufacturing issues.

Therefore, use the **Fillet** tool to first add six 5mm Fillets to the six upright edges of the hexagon.

5. Next, add a 2mm Fillet to both the top and bottom edges of the hexagon, as illustrated in *Figure 10.15*. Note that creating an initial base that was larger than the tool shape now allows us to easily add the lower Fillet. Without the base, it would be much more difficult to create the lower, filleted edge:

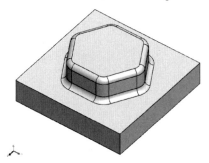

Figure 10.15: Adding Fillets to remove sharp edges

Now that we have a filleted lower edge, we no longer need the initial base feature, and so we can cut this away.

6. Expand the first `Boss-Extrude` feature and select the sketch underneath. Then, use this sketch to create an Extruded Cut that is the same depth as the first `Boss-Extrude` feature (10mm), completely cutting away the first `Boss-Extrude` feature, as illustrated in *Figure 10.16*.

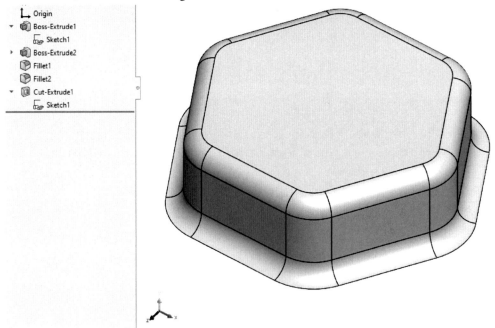

Figure 10.16: Cutting away the initial base, using the first sketch and a Cut Extrude

The geometry of our tool is now complete, but before converting it into a Forming Tool, we can add an *Orientation Sketch*. This sketch can be used in **Flat Pattern** versions of models and can also be helpful when positioning a *part*.

7. Start a sketch on the underside face of the tool. Then, left-click to select the entire face and press the **Convert Entities** tool (on the **Sketch** tab). This will convert the outline of the face into new sketch entities, giving an outline of the tool.

8. Next, select the **Point** tool and add a *point* at the center of the tool (lined up with Origin). This can be used to help position the tool.

    Then, exit the sketch.

    You can see an outline of the tool in *Figure 10.17*):

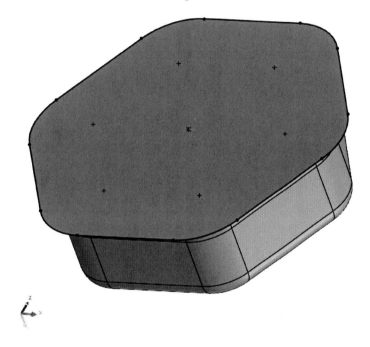

Figure 10.17: Adding an Orientation Sketch

9. We are now ready to convert the *part* to a Forming Tool.

    Select **Insert | Sheet Metal | Forming Tool**, and the **Form Tool Property Manager** will open.

10. Select the **Stopping Face** field.

This is the face of the tool that will stop at the face of the sheet where the tool is inserted. In other words, it is the face of the tool that will be coplanar (lined up) with the metal sheet when the tool is at its deepest point. *Figure 10.18* shows an example of this on a different tool:

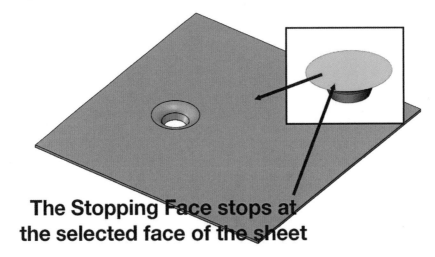

The Stopping Face stops at
the selected face of the sheet

Figure 10.18: The Stopping Face

Select the underside face of the tool (the same face where the Orientation Sketch was drawn). Note that it turns cyan.

11. Next, the **Faces to Remove** field can be set.

This selection is optional; it's not necessary to remove any faces, but any that are selected here will turn red and will be cut out of the sheet when the Forming Tool is used.

Select the upper face of the tool, as illustrated in *Figure 10.19*.

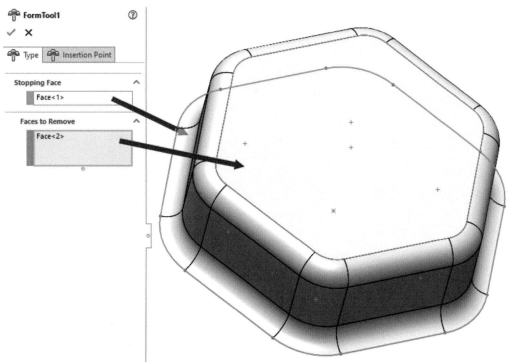

Figure 10.19: Selecting the upper face as the Face to Remove

Note that faces can also be split into smaller faces (by drawing sketch entities, such as lines and circles, on the areas to be split up and then using the **Split Line** tool) if you only want to cut away certain sections of a flat face, rather than the entire face.

12. Finally, we can set the **Insertion Point** field by selecting that tab in the **Property Manager**, and then selecting the *point* from the Orientation Sketch (or the Origin; both should be in the same place).

13. Press the green **OK** check mark to create a **Form Tool** feature (*Figure 10.20*). Note that the feature appears in the FeatureManager Design Tree and the tool in the Graphics Area is now color-coded. As previously mentioned, yellow indicates bend faces, red indicates faces that will be removed, and cyan (underneath) shows the Stopping Face:

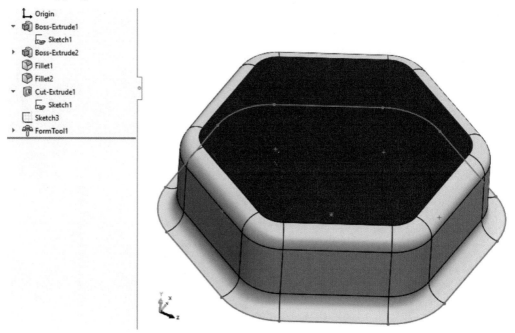

Figure 10.20: The created Form Tool

14. Before use, the Forming Tool has to be saved. There are two main ways to do this, as outlined here:

- **Save as a part document**: The document can be saved as a standard *part* file (with a *.SLDPRT file extension). If the *part* is saved within the forming tools folder, then SolidWorks will recognize it as a Forming Tool, even if it is saved as a standard *part* file. If the file is saved in a different location, then SolidWorks will not recognize the *part* as a Forming Tool.

- **Save as a Forming Tool document**: Alternatively, the model can be saved as a specific Forming Tool file (with a *.SLDFTP file extension). In this case, the file can be saved in any location and SolidWorks will still recognize it as a Forming Tool.

> **Forming Tool or Part Document?**
>
> Forming Tools can be saved as either file type, as detailed previously. The difference between the two is mostly just a matter of file organization. If you prefer to keep all files from a specific project in the same location, then it may be best to save the tool as a Forming Tool document (`*.SLDFTP`), but if the Forming Tool is a generic tool that will be used on multiple projects, then you may prefer to save it directly into the **Design Library** as a normal *part* file.

Save the tool file by going to **File | Save As…**.

The type of document can then be set by selecting from the **Save as type** drop-down menu, directly underneath the filename.

In this case, save the tool as a standard SolidWorks *part*, within the `forming tools` folder. (The default location is `C:\ProgramData\SolidWorks\ SolidWorks 20xx\Design Library\Forming Tools`.)

15. After saving, open the **Design Library** within the **Task Pane** on the right-hand side of the screen and check that your new tool appears with the other Forming Tools. It can now be dragged into models and used in the same way as the standard Forming Tools.

    If the tool does not appear, you may need to add it to the **Design Library** using the **Add to library** button, as described in the information box at the end of the *Modifying existing forming tools* section.

> **Forming Tool Not Working Correctly?**
>
> If you find that your new Forming Tool does not work correctly, then try checking that the corners are rounded. Sharp corners can sometimes cause errors with Forming Tools.

This section showed how to create entirely Custom Forming Tools instead of just modifying existing models. This greatly expands the range of indentations and cuts that you can use.

Summary

In this chapter, we looked at how to use the Forming Tools from the **Design Library** to add 3D detail to your Sheet Metal models. We also explored modifying existing tools to suit your own needs, as well as creating completely Custom Forming Tools. This allows a virtually unlimited variety of Forming Tool shapes and sizes to be used.

In the next chapter, we will learn how existing 3D models can be converted into Sheet Metal models using the **Insert Bends** tool.

Section 3:
Converting 3D Parts to Sheet Metal and Creating a Sheet Metal Enclosure

As well as creating Sheet Metal models from scratch, we can also convert existing 3D designs into Sheet Metal models. This section shows two different ways to do this, and also provides a practical example that brings together a number of the skills that we have learned throughout the book.

This section contains the following chapters:

11
Converting to Sheet Metal Using the Insert Bends Tool

3D models with a constant wall thickness (for example, *Shelled* or *Thin Feature* parts), can be converted into Sheet Metal *parts* by using the **Insert Bends** tool. This chapter shows how to use this tool to create Sheet Metal parts.

By the end of this chapter, learners will be able to confidently use the Insert Bends tool.

In this chapter, we're going to cover the following main topics:

- Using the Insert Bends tool with Shelled parts
- Using the Insert Bends tool with Thin Feature parts

Using the Insert Bends tool with Shelled parts

So far in the book, we have covered most of the **SolidWorks Sheet Metal** tools, and in almost every case, we have started our models using the **Base Flange** feature. However, it's also possible to convert existing solid models into Sheet Metal models. This can be done in two main ways: by using the **Insert Bends** tool or by using the **Convert to Sheet Metal** tool. While these two tools are similar, they do have some important differences, which will be explained in this chapter and *Chapter 12, Building Sheet Metal Parts Using the Convert to Sheet Metal Tool,* respectively.

> **Should I Use a Base Flange or Convert a Solid Model to Sheet Metal?**
>
> Generally, starting a Sheet Metal model using a Base Flange is the better option, because it gives you flexibility if changes are required at a later stage. At times, it may seem like creating a solid model and then converting it to Sheet Metal will be faster, but in the long run, once any future modifications are taken into account, it is often better to start with a Base Flange.
>
> The Insert Bends and Convert to Sheet Metal tools are generally more useful when working with pre-existing models that you may have received from a different source, or previously made yourself.

The Insert Bends tool allows us to convert solid models – such as Shelled or Thin Feature *parts* – to Sheet Metal *parts*. It works best with *parts* that have a uniform (that is, constant) wall thickness. If your model is completely solid or has a variable wall thickness then it is usually better to use the Convert to Sheet Metal tool, which is covered in *Chapter 12, Building Sheet Metal Parts Using the Convert to Sheet Metal Tool.*

To demonstrate the use of the Insert Bends tool, first, we are going to create a simple Shelled model:

1. Start a new *part* document and create a solid cube that is 100 mm long on each side. This can be made by sketching a Center Rectangle on the Top Plane, then using the **Extruded Boss/Base** tool and the Mid Plane End Condition.

2. Hollow out the cube and remove the upper face by selecting the **Shell** tool and selecting the upper face as one of the **Faces to Remove** (*Figure 11.1*). Set the wall thickness as **2mm**.

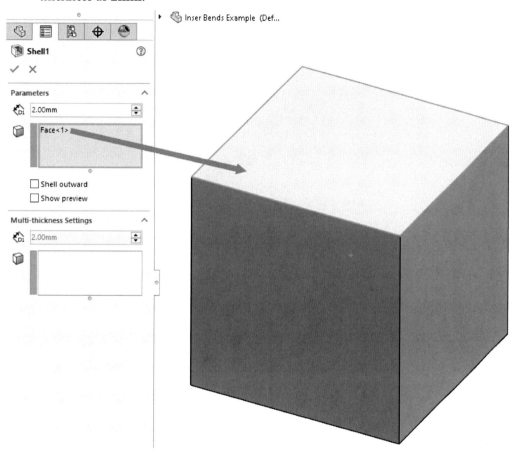

Figure 11.1: Shelling the cube to a wall thickness of 2 mm and removing the upper face

3. Now, if we go to a **Section View** we can see that the cube has a constant 2 mm wall thickness all the way around (*Figure 11.2*). This makes it ideal for converting to Sheet Metal by using the **Insert Bends** feature.

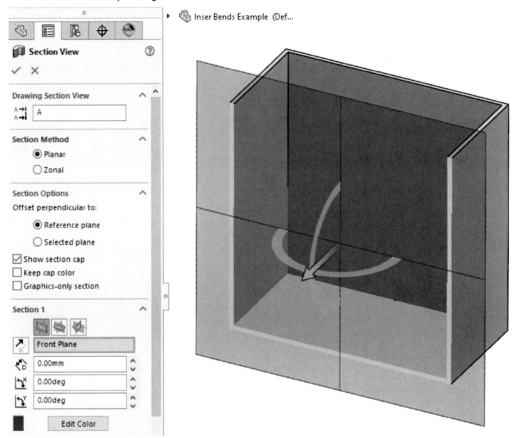

Figure 11.2: The cube has a constant wall thickness

4. Close the **Section View** and select the **Insert Bends** tool from the **Sheet Metal** tab or toolbar.

The **Insert Bends** Property Manager appears (*Figure 11.3*). We can use this to set the default parameters of the Sheet Metal *part* (such as the Bend Radius and Auto Relief). Note that the Thickness setting is unavailable because the thickness is determined by the actual thickness of the solid part.

Set a Bend Radius of **2mm** and keep the other settings as the default values.

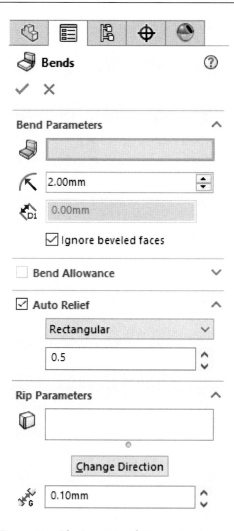

Figure 11.3: The Insert Bends Property Manager

5. Once the parameters have been set, we need to select a **Fixed Face or Edge**. This will be the face or edge that does not move and it can be thought of as similar to a **Base Flange**.

Spin the cube over and select the underside face as the Fixed Face (*Figure 11.4*).

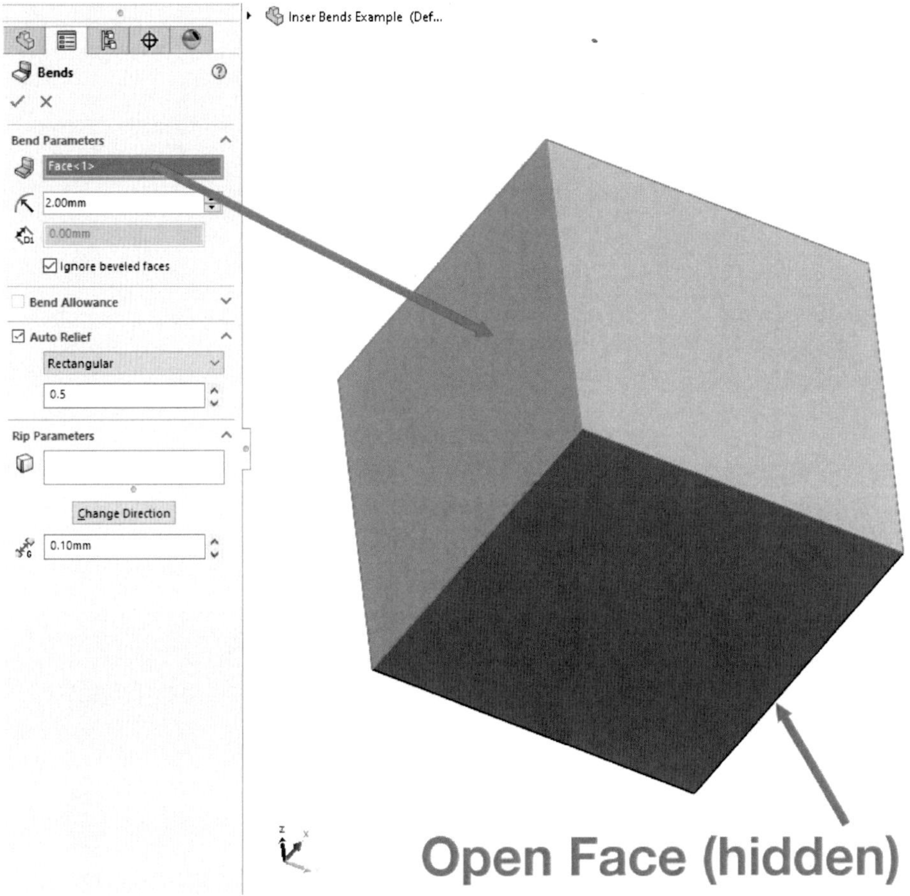

Figure 11.4: Selecting the underside face as the Fixed Face

6. Before clicking the **OK** check mark, we must first select the **Edges to Rip** in the **Rip Parameters** section.

To convert this 3D design to a flat sheet, we need to unfold the vertical sides of the cube. However, they are currently joined together. Therefore, certain edges must be *ripped* to allow the sides of the cube to be unfolded. If we think of the cube as if it was a real-life object (for example, if it was made out of cardboard), we would have to rip down the four vertical edges before we could unfold the side faces. Therefore, we need to select these edges in the **Rip Parameters** section.

Left-click the box under **Rip Parameters** to select the **Edges to Rip** box, then, select the four vertical edges of the cube. Notice that yellow arrows will appear on each of the selected edges (*Figure 11.5*). These arrows indicate the direction of the *rip*.

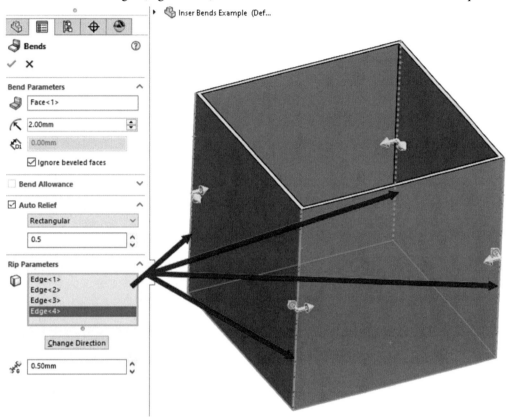

Figure 11.5: Selecting the four vertical edges to rip

7. We can also set the **Rip Gap** distance by adjusting the value at the bottom of the **Rip Parameters** section. Set this to **0.5mm**.

8. Click the green **OK** check mark to create the Insert Bends feature. You may receive a message telling you that Auto Relief cuts were made for one or more of the bends.

The part is now converted to a Sheet Metal part and a number of features appear in the FeatureManager Design Tree (*Figure 11.6*). We can also see that the lower edges that were previously sharp have now been converted to bends and that Auto Relief cuts have been added to the lower corners.

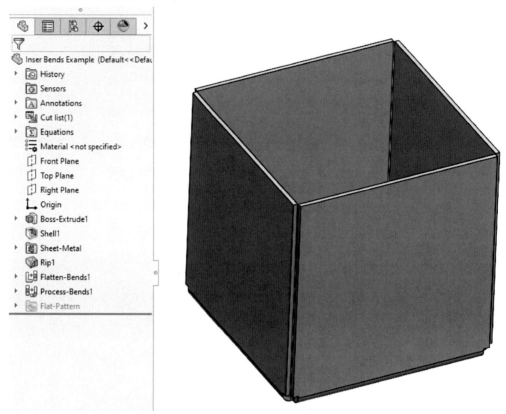

Figure 11.6: The Insert Bends features and model

Looking at the FeatureManager Design Tree (on the left-hand side of *Figure 11.6*) shows us a step-by-step guide of the process that has just occurred.

First, we created the cube shape (**Boss-Extrude1**) and Shelled it out (**Shell1**). Next, the Sheet-Metal folder was added as part of the Insert Bends process. As usual, this folder always contains all of the Sheet Metal parameters for this *part*. This is followed by the Rip feature (**Rip1**) that cut rips down the vertical edges of the cube. The Flatten-Bends operation (**Flatten-Bends1**) then folded down the sides of the cube, and the Process-Bends operation (**Process-Bends1**) added the bends into the model and folded the sides back up. Finally, the Flat-Pattern folder was added, and this will allow us to flatten the part at a future stage if needed. If we do flatten the model (*Figure 11.7*), the relief cuts in the corners will be seen much more easily.

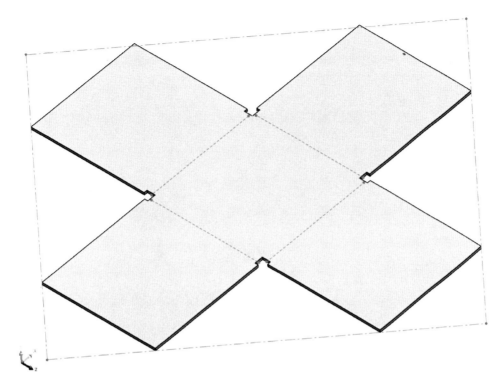

Figure 11.7: The flattened model, showing the relief cuts in the corners

The Rollback Bar (the blue horizontal bar at the bottom of the FeatureManager Design Tree) can be dragged up through these features, allowing you to step back through the model and see these changes one by one.

Adjusting Rips

When using the Insert Bends tool, we can also adjust the rips to specify their direction. This can be done either when you are initially creating the feature or at a later stage by editing the Rip feature:

1. Ensure that your model is in an unflattened state.

2. Left or right click on the Rip feature in the FeatureManager Design Tree and select **Edit Feature**.

3. The rip direction can be changed by selecting an edge and then clicking the **Change Direction** button in the Property Manager on the left, or it can be changed by clicking on the yellow arrows in the Graphics Area (*Figure 11.8*).

Rips can be in either of the single directions (left or right) or they can be in *both directions* at the same time. However, clicking on the yellow direction-arrows can only reverse the single-direction options. To set the rip edge to *both directions*, it must be selected in the **Edges to Rip** box and then changed by clicking the **Change Direction** button to cycle between the three different states.

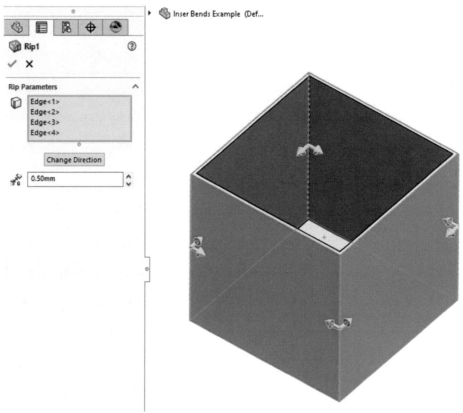

Figure 11.8: Adjusting the rip directions

4.   The Rip Gap distance can also be adjusted in the Property Manager.

5.   Press the green **OK** check mark to accept any changes.

It is also possible to use the Rip tool independently of the Insert Bends tool by selecting the **Rip** tool. This might be helpful if your model needs further operations after the rips but before any bends are added. However, it usually makes sense to combine the operations directly by just using the Insert Bends tool.

So far, we have looked at how to create Sheet Metal models from *Shelled* parts with a constant wall thickness, but the Insert Bends tool can also be used with *Thin Feature* models.·

Using the Insert Bends tool with Thin Feature parts

Shelled models are reasonably common when working with SolidWorks, however, you may also encounter models that are *open* but not *entirely flat*. These could be items such as simple mounting brackets. In these cases, the Insert Bends tool can still be used to convert these models into Sheet Metal *parts*:

1. Start a new SolidWorks part document and start a sketch on the Right Plane.

2. Use the **Line** tool to draw the sketch shown in *Figure 11.9*.

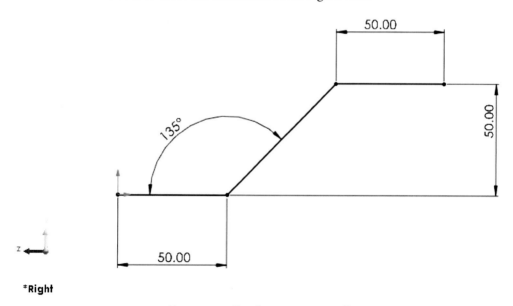

Figure 11.9: Sketching an open profile

3. Use the sketch to create an Extruded Boss/Base. This can be 50 mm long, with a Blind End Condition. Ensure that you also select the **Thin Feature** option if it is not already selected (this should be automatically selected when trying to extrude an open profile), and then set the thickness to **Mid-Plane** and **2mm** thick (*Figure 11.10*). Next, click **OK** check mark to create the feature.

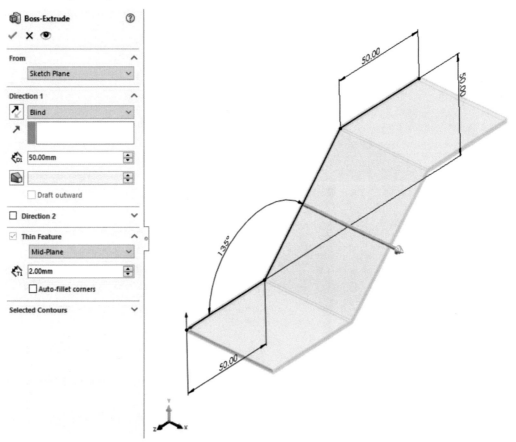

Figure 11.10: Extrude the sketch using Thin Feature

4. This part can now be converted into a Sheet Metal *part* by selecting the **Insert Bends** tool.

5. As before, we now need to set the model's parameters and select a Fixed Face or Edge. Set the Bend Radius as 2 mm and select the lower, horizontal face (the one that is fixed to the Origin) as the **Fixed Face or Edge**. In this case, we don't need to rip any edges, so the **Rip Parameters** section can be ignored.

6. Press the green **OK** check mark to create the feature. It can now be seen that the model is converted to a Sheet Metal *part* and the Flatten Bends and Process Bends features are added to the FeatureManager Design Tree. Note that even though we sketched a profile with sharp corners, these have automatically been converted to 2 mm bends (*Figure 11.11*), according to the Bend Radius value that we set in *Step 5*.

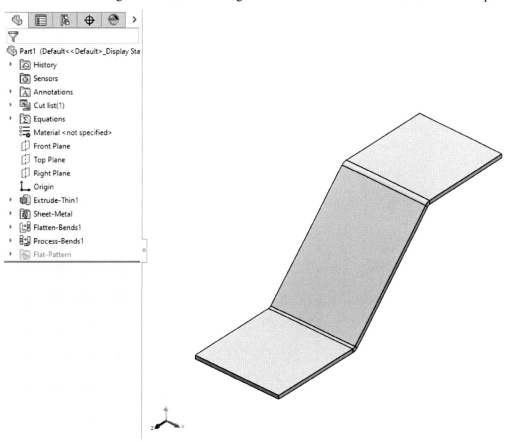

Figure 11.11: The model is converted to a Sheet Metal part

If you were to actually create the model that we have just used in this example, it would usually be much better to use a Base Flange and Edge Flanges. However, there may be cases that are similar but more complicated, or you may have been sent a model by a different person, or even in a different file format. In these instances, it may be best to use the Insert Bends tool to convert models directly to Sheet Metal parts.

Summary

In this chapter, we looked at converting 3D models into Sheet Metal parts by using the Insert Bends tool. This tool is especially useful when working with solid models that have a constant wall thickness, such as *Shelled* parts. It can also be used to save time if you already have existing models that need to be turned into Sheet Metal versions, or have simple Thin Feature models.

It is also possible to convert models by using the dedicated **Convert to Sheet Metal** tool, and we will explore this in the next chapter.

12
Building Sheet Metal Parts Using the Convert to Sheet Metal Tool

The **Convert to Sheet Metal** tool can be used to turn existing Solid models into Sheet Metal *parts*. It is especially useful when those models don't have a constant wall thickness. The tool is quite versatile and has a number of options which are explained in detail here.

In this chapter we're going to cover the following main topics:

- Using the **Convert to Sheet Metal** tool
- **Convert to Sheet Metal** – Advanced Options
- Solving conversion issues

Using the Convert to Sheet Metal tool

The **Convert to Sheet Metal** tool is quite similar to the **Insert Bends** tool that we introduced in the previous chapter in that it can be useful for converting preexisting solid models into Sheet Metal models. It differs from the **Insert Bends** tool because it can be used with bodies that are completely solid, instead of those with a regular wall thickness. This can be a great time-saver if you have been sent models by external clients or partners who are working with different CAD systems.

To demonstrate how to use the tool, first, we will create a simple, solid shape:

1. Start a new SolidWorks *part* document and sketch the profile shown in *Figure 12.1* on the Front Plane.

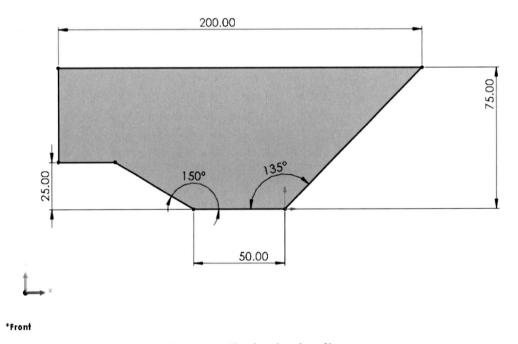

Figure 12.1: Sketch a closed profile

2. Extrude the shape 75mm, using the **Extruded Boss/Base** and the **Mid Plane** End Condition (*Figure 12.2*).

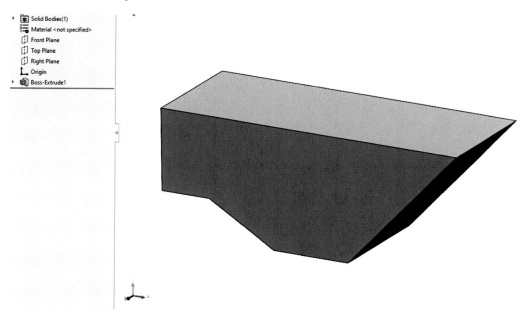

Figure 12.2: Extrude the sketch

3. Select the **Convert to Sheet Metal** tool. A large number of options now appear in the Property Manager.

4. The workflow is quite similar to the **Insert Bends** tool from the previous chapter. First, we need to set the parameters that we will use for the Sheet Metal *part,* and then select a **Fixed Face** (*Figure 12.3*).

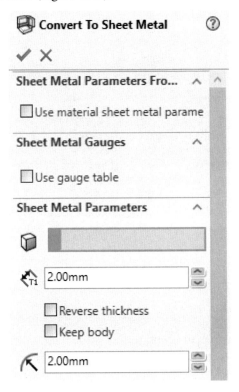

Figure 12.3: Setting the Sheet Metal parameters

5. Set the **Thickness** as 2mm (the **Gauge Tables** can also be used by ticking the **Use gauge table** box) and the **Bend Radius** as 2mm. Leave the **Reverse thickness** and **Keep body** boxes unchecked.

6. Next, select the **Fixed Entity**. This will be the face or edge that doesn't move when the model is unbent. It can be thought of as similar to the **Base Flange** in normal Sheet Metal *parts.*

7. Rotate the model and select the lowest underside face as the **Fixed Entity** (*Figure 12.4*).

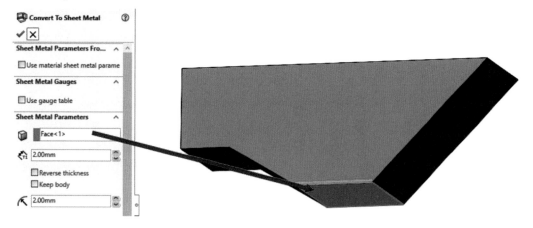

Figure 12.4: Select the Fixed Entity

8. Next, we must select the edges where we'd like to add bends. Click in the **Bend Edges** selection box and then select the two edges shown in *Figure 12.5*.

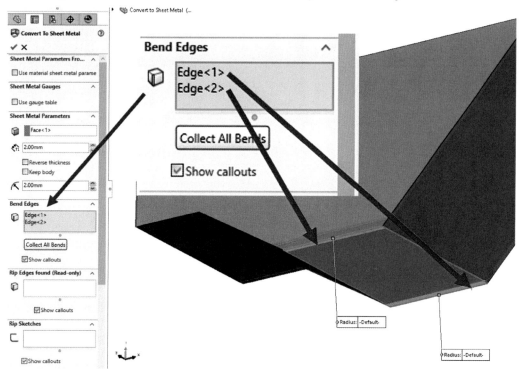

Figure 12.5: Select the edges to bend

9. Now create the **Convert to Sheet Metal** feature by pressing the green **OK** check mark.

10. We can see that the solid has been converted to a Sheet Metal *part* with a thickness of 2mm that we set in *Step 4*. 2mm bends have been added to the two selected edges. Also, note all of the faces connected to edges that were not selected have been removed from the model (*Figure 12.6*).

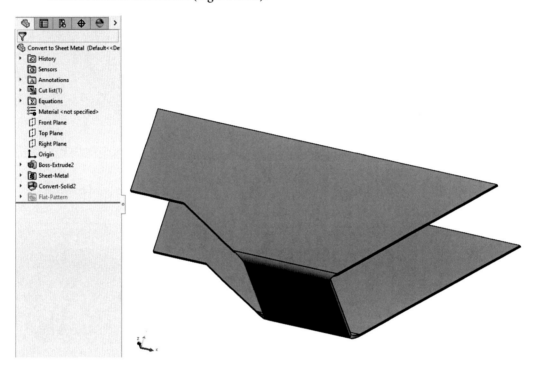

Figure 12.6: The converted part

11. The FeatureManager Design Tree on the left-hand side of the screen now includes the **Sheet-Metal** and **Flat-Pattern** folders, indicating that this *part* is a Sheet Metal model. It also contains the **Convert-Solid** feature itself. Edit the feature by clicking on **Convert-Solid** and selecting **Edit Feature**.

12. We will now add further **Bend Edges** and look at how **Rip Edges** can be used. Keep the two existing **Bend Edges** and add a third edge, as shown in *Figure 12.7*.

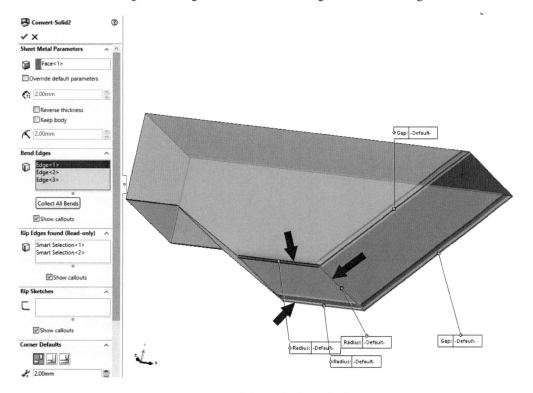

Figure 12.7: Select a third Bend Edge

13. Notice that the **Rip Edges** selection box has now been automatically filled by the two edges highlighted in pink in *Figure 12.7*. This selection is automatic because if we create bends at the three locations that we have selected then the pink edges must be ripped, otherwise, the bend faces wouldn't be able to fold flat.

14. Press the green **OK** check mark to update the feature and note that the Sheet Metal model now contains the additional face related to the third bend that we selected (*Figure 12.8*). The pink edges from Step 10 have also been ripped, that is, they have a small gap.

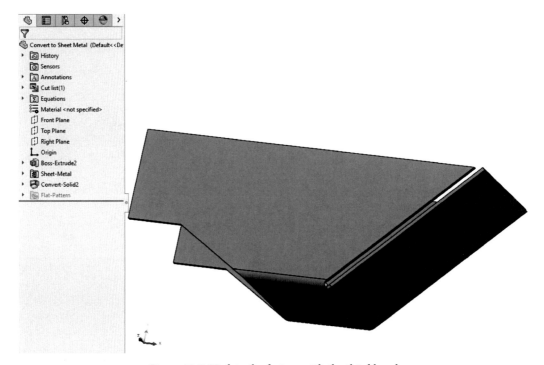

Figure 12.8: Update the feature with the third bend

Depending on which **Bend Edges** we select, we may create 3D models that look similar but have quite different footprints. It is usually worth thinking about exactly what you want to achieve from your model before selecting the bends.

To show an example:

1. Edit the **Convert Solid** feature again so that we are back in the tool's Property Manager.

2. Clear all of the selections in the **Bend Edges** selection box and select the three edges shown in *Figure 12.9*.

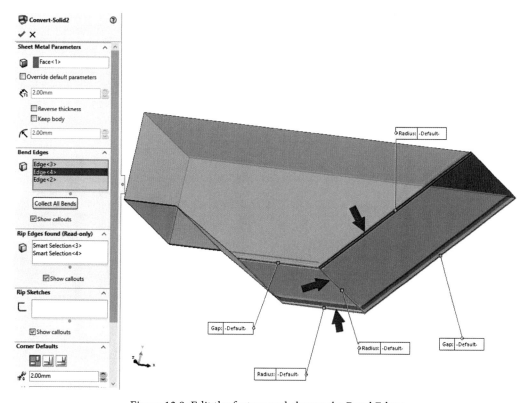

Figure 12.9: Edit the feature and change the Bend Edges

3. Press **OK** to accept the changes. We can now see that although this new shape and the shape from *Figure 12.8* appear very similar in 3D, they are completely different when Flattened (*Figure 12.10*).

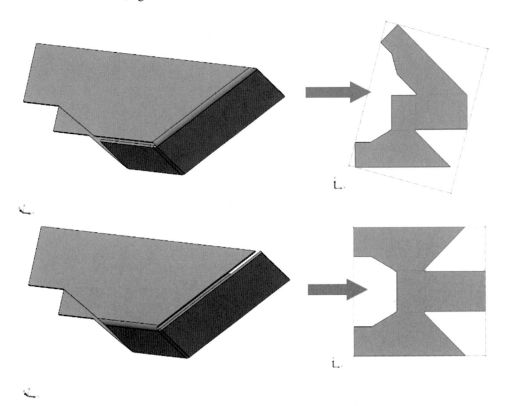

Figure 12.10: Different Bend Edge selections can give very variable results.

One final important aspect of using the **Convert to Sheet Metal** tool is that bends have to be selected in order:

1. Edit the **Convert Solid** feature again so that we are back in the tool's Property Manager.

2. Clear all of the selections in the **Bend Edges** selection box. Then select the five edges in the order shown in *Figure 12.11*. If you try to select an edge that is not connected to the Fixed Face (for example, if you try to select Edge 4 before selecting Edge 3) then a warning will pop up; edges must be selected in the correct order so that they are connected to the Fixed Face.

3. After selecting Edge 5 note that the **Rip Edges** automatically appears on the top-right edge.

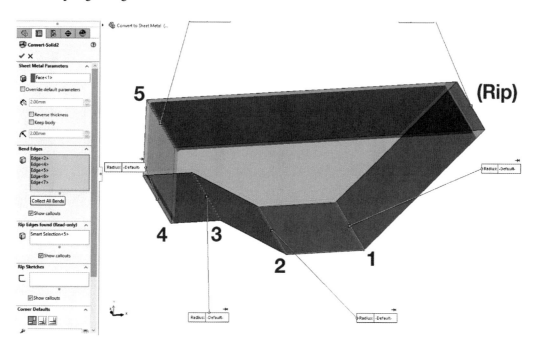

Figure 12.11: Select the five Bend Edges shown

4. Select the two further edges shown in *Figure 12.12* and note that **Rip Edges** are automatically applied all the way around the large faces of the shape.

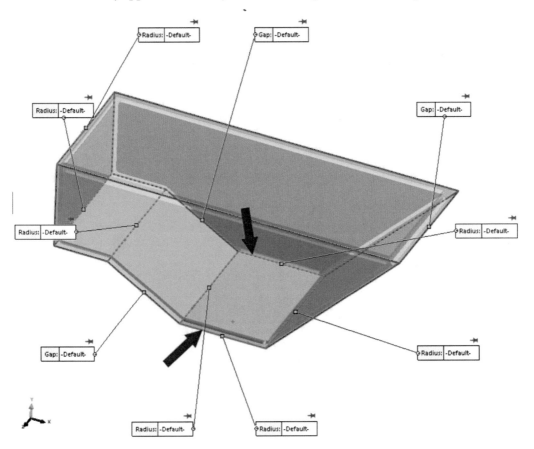

Figure 12.12: Select the final two Bend Edges

5. Press the green **OK** check mark to update the feature and we can now see that the entire shape has been converted to a Sheet Metal *part*. This is shown in *Figure 12.13* in both a Flattened and Unflattened state.

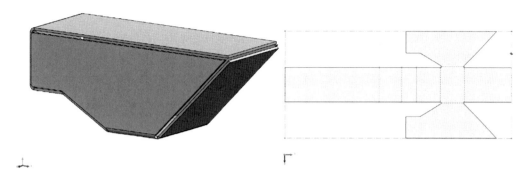

Figure 12.13: The completed part

This section showed how to use the basic functions of the **Convert to Sheet Metal** tool but there are a number of more advanced settings that can be used to fine-tune your Sheet Metal shapes.

Convert to Sheet Metal – Advanced Options

Now that we understand how to use the **Convert to Sheet Metal** tool let's look at the **Reverse Thickness**, **Keep Body**, **Manual Rip Sketches**, and **Corner Defaults** options in more detail.

Reverse Thickness option

This setting allows the direction of the newly-created sheets to be reversed:

1. Continuing from the previous section, edit the **Convert Solid** feature again, so that we are back in the tool's Property Manager.

2. We can now see two options under the Sheet Metal Parameters – **Reverse thickness** and **Keep body** (*Figure 12.14*).

Figure 12.14: The Sheet Metal Parameters

3. Put a check mark in the **Reverse thickness** box and watch the preview in the Graphics Area closely. You should see that the size of the previewed part increases slightly so that the new, added sheets will be *outside* of the original shape, rather than completely enclosed within it. Try toggling the **Reverse thickness** option on and off to have a closer look at the changes.

4. Select the **Reverse thickness** option (put a check mark in the box), then press **OK** to accept the changes. If we now measure the outside size of the *part* we can see that it is 79mm. This is the size of the original shape (75mm), plus the thickness of the two extra outer sheets (2mm each), on each side.

5. The **Reverse thickness** option is a very simple setting but one that can be very useful if the internal size of your model is important.

The Keep body option

Usually when a solid body is converted to Sheet Metal the original solid body is consumed (used up) by the **Convert to Sheet Metal** feature. However, there may be cases where we want to retain the original body. For example, we might want to reuse it to create another sheet:

1. Continuing from the previous subsection, edit the **Convert Solid** feature again, so that we are back in the tool's Property Manager.

2. Select the **Keep body** option (*Figure 12.14*).

3. Press **OK** to accept the changes. We can now see that the new Sheet Metal feature has been added, but the original body still remains in the model (*Figure 12.15*). If you still have the **Reverse thickness** option selected then we will also see that the Sheet Metal feature is larger than the original body.

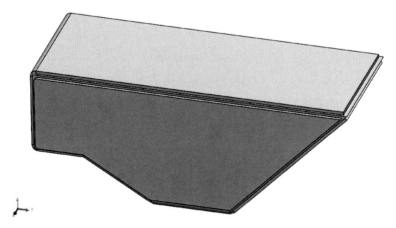

Figure 12.15: Selecting the Keep body option keeps the original body in the model

We can also see that the Cut list folder in the FeatureManager Design Tree (*Figure 12.16*) is now followed by a **(2)**. This indicates that we have two sheets or bodies in the current model. Expanding the folder allows us to see each of these in turn and they can be shown or hidden by selecting the item and clicking **Show** or **Hide**.

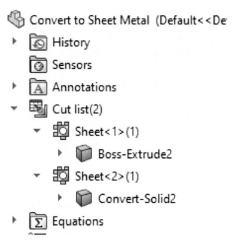

Figure 12.16: The Cut list folder displays sheets and bodies in a model

4. The **Keep body** option can be especially useful if you want to use a single body to create two or more sheets.

5. Continuing from the previous subsection, edit the **Convert Solid** feature again, so that we are back in the tool's Property Manager.

6. Ensure that the **Keep body** and **Reverse thickness** options are still both selected but adjust the **Bend Edges** so only the five edges shown in *Figure 12.17* are selected.

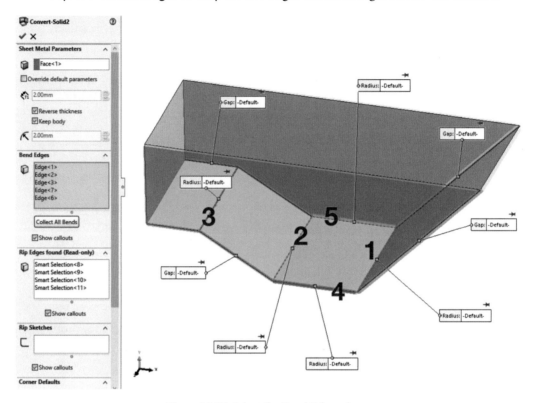

Figure 12.17: Select the Bend Edges shown

7. Press **OK** to accept the changes. Now we can see that we have a Sheet Metal sheet with no top and left-hand edge and we also have the original solid body (*Figure 12.18*).

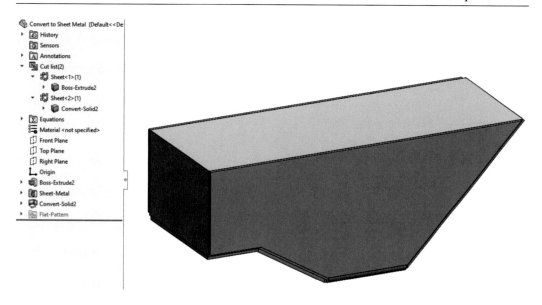

Figure 12.18: The sheet and original body

8. We can now reuse the solid body to create a second sheet. Select the **Convert to Sheet Metal** tool again.

9. This time select the upper face of the original body as the Fixed Face and the upper edge shown in *Figure 12.19* as the Bend Line.

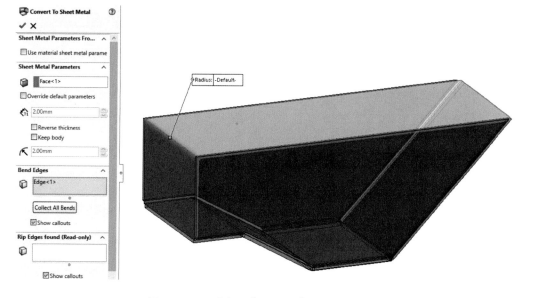

Figure 12.19: Select the upper face and the edge

10. Deselect the **Keep body** option because we no longer need to keep the body. Also, deselect the **Reverse thickness** option. This will mean that this new sheet will fit within the first sheet and is a good example of why **Reverse thickness** can be useful for creating multi-sheet *parts* that fit together properly.

11. Press **OK** to create the second sheet. *Figure 12.20* shows both sheets in an exploded view and shows how **Keep body** can be used with a single solid model to create *parts* with multiple sheets.

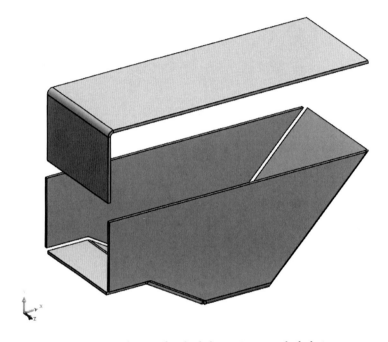

Figure 12.20: The two finished sheets, in an exploded view

As well as creating multi-sheet models, there may also be instances where it's not desirable to create rips at existing edges. In these cases, manual **Rip Lines** can be used.

Manual Rip Lines

So far we have just used the automatically allocated Rip Lines when converting to Sheet Metal. However, there may be times when we need to specify exactly where faces will be split apart using rips:

1. Continue from the previous subsection, but delete the two existing **Convert Solid** features and the **Sheet-Metal folder** so that we only have the first **Boss-Extrude** in the model.

2. Manual **Rip Lines** must be sketched *before* the **Convert to Sheet Metal** feature. In this case, we deleted the previous **Convert to Sheet Metal** features, but it is also possible to drag the **Rollback Bar** above the **Convert-Solid** feature in models and add sketches at that stage.

3. Now sketch the **Rip Lines** using the **Line Tool**. For this example start a sketch on the large, upper face of the shape and draw a line directly between the midpoints of the long edges (*Figure 12.21*). Then exit the sketch.

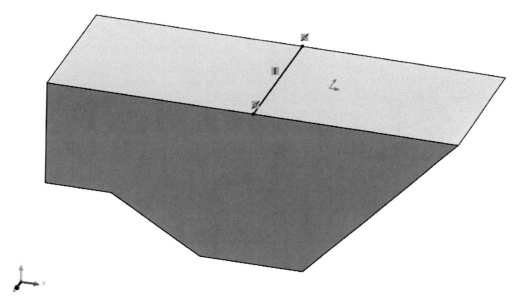

Figure 12.21: Sketch the Rip Line

4. We can now add the **Convert to Sheet Metal** feature as covered earlier in the chapter. Select the **Convert to Sheet Metal** tool, then select the underside face as the **Fixed Face**, then select the **Bend Edges** shown in *Figure 12.22*.

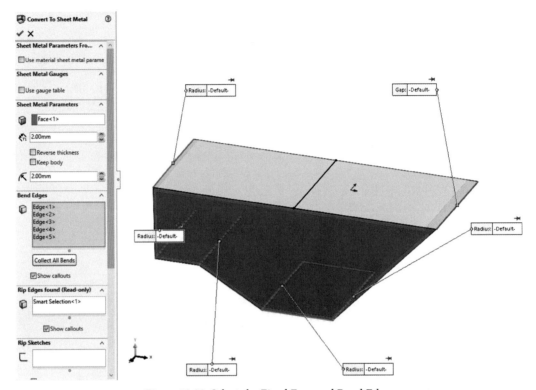

Figure 12.22: Select the Fixed Face and Bend Edges

5. Note that **Rip Edge** has still been automatically selected as the upper-right edge. However, we can manually change this to our Rip Sketch. To do this, click in the **Rip Sketches** selection box in the Property Manager, then select the Rip Sketch that we drew in Step 3 (*Figure 12.23*).

If you have difficulty selecting the actual line in the Graphics Area then it can be easier to expand the second Design Tree (in the upper left of the Graphics Area) and select the entire sketch there.

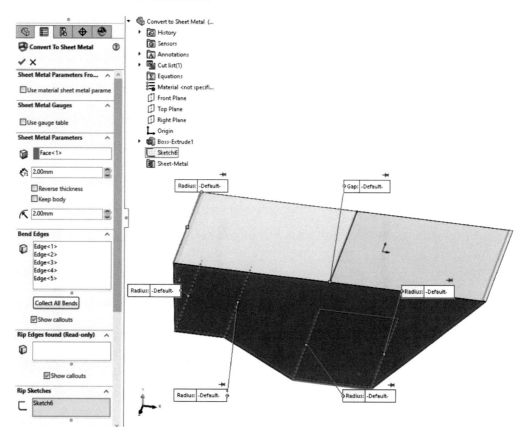

Figure 12.23: Select the Rip Sketch

6. We can now see that the upper face will be ripped along the Rip Sketch and that the top-right edge is no longer selected for a bend.

Add the top-right edge to the **Bend Edges**.

7. Press **OK** to create the feature and note that the **Rip Line** is halfway along the top edge (*Figure 12.24*).

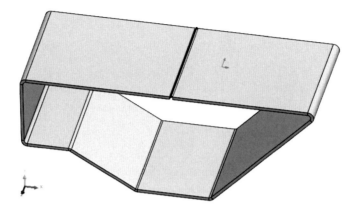

Figure 12.24: The finished model with a manual rip

This method of adding manual Rip Lines can be extremely useful for specifying exactly how your solid parts will be created. There are also a number of smaller rip details that can be changed.

Adjusting rip and corner details

Rip details can be further specified within the Property Manager of the **Convert-Solid** feature (*Figure 12.25*). Here, is it possible to change the style of the corner (**Butt, Underlap,** or **Overlap**), to adjust the **Gap Distance,** and to adjust the **Overlap/ Underlap Ratios**.

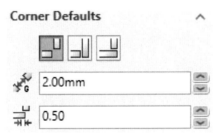

Figure 12.25: Corner Defaults

It's also possible to adjust the details of each bend and rip individually by selecting them in the Graphics Area and making any required changes.

When creating Sheet Metal models using the **Convert to Sheet Metal** tool sometimes problematic features may accidentally be created. In the next section, we will look at an example of this and how it can be overcome.

Solving conversion issues

When creating standard Sheet Metal models starting from a **Base Flange** it is generally quite difficult to create new flanges that have flattening issues, because SolidWorks will often automatically trim away problem areas. However, sometimes when converting models to Sheet Metal these flattening issues can occur inadvertently. We can force SolidWorks to create one of these issues, as an example of how to avoid it:

1. Continuing from the previous section, edit the **Convert Solid** feature again, so that we are back in the tool's Property Manager.

2. Change the Fixed Face from the small underside face to the large side face (*Figure 12.26*). Then remove any existing **Bend Edges** (this will automatically remove any Rip Edges, if it does not then delete these manually) and just add the three **Bend Edges** shown.

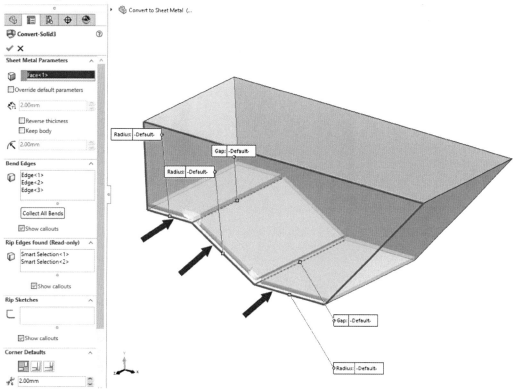

Figure 12.26: Adjust the Convert Solid feature

3. Press **OK** to update the feature.

4. If we now rotate the model we can see that everything appears correct in 3D and no errors are visible. However, if we attempt to **Flatten** the model by pressing the **Flatten** button we can now see that two of the flanges occupy the same position (*Figure 12.27*).

Note
Depending on your SolidWorks version your model may not flatten but instead may display an error.

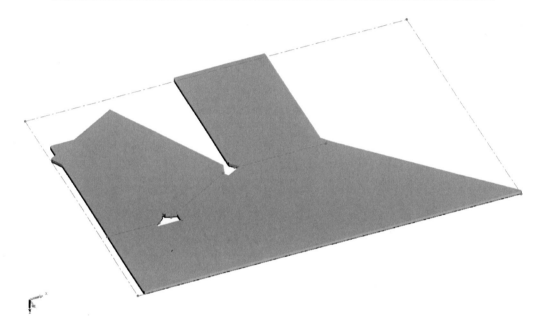

Figure 12.27: Two of the flattened flanges occupy the same space

It would be impossible to make this model (as it currently is) in real life because two different sections of it cannot come from the same area of flat sheet. This doesn't necessarily mean that the overall part cannot be made, just that we might have to create it in a slightly different way, perhaps by adjusting where the bends are placed.

> **If Your Model Does Not Flatten**
>
> If you find that your models do not **Flatten** correctly then expand the **Flat-Pattern** Folder and look for any error or warning messages. This will indicate which features have problems that need to be fixed. If no errors are visible but the model still doesn't **Flatten** then try suppressing earlier features, one by one, and then, if your model does not **Flatten** until you can narrow it down to a single problem area.

One of the limitations of SolidWorks, and 3D CAD in general, is that sometimes models can be created using a computer that cannot be actually made in real life. When modeling, try to always consider how your parts will actually be made, and this can help reduce this kind of issue.

Summary

In this chapter we looked at converting 3D models into Sheet Metal *parts* by using the **Convert to Sheet Metal** tool. We explored many of the sub-options and briefly discussed errors that might occur, and how they can be fixed. The **Convert to Sheet Metal** tool is a great option for saving time by taking pre-existing models and quickly changing them into a Sheet Metal format.

In the next chapter, we will put together many of the techniques that we learned about in earlier chapters, and use them to create a sheet metal enclosure.

13
Practical Example: The Sheet Metal Enclosure

Sheet metal enclosures are common in the electronics industry. This chapter shows how to use various Sheet Metal techniques that we have learned to create an example enclosure, as well as giving handy tips and tricks for practical modeling. In this chapter, we're going to cover the following main topics:

- Creating the enclosure base

- Adding more details to the enclosure

- Creating an enclosure lid

- Adding final details to the enclosure

These sections will show how the various Sheet Metal tools can be used to build up a complete project. By the end of the chapter, you will know how SolidWorks Sheet Metal can be utilized in a real-world design situation.

Creating the enclosure base

Our example enclosure will consist of two components – the *base* and the *lid* – both made within the same SolidWorks *part* file. These will each be made as separate sheets within the *part* file, starting off with the base sheet.

Throughout this chapter, the instructions given are more of a guide than hard-and-fast parameters, so feel free to experiment with different sizes and features as you see fit.

To create the base, follow these steps:

1. Start a new SolidWorks *part* document.

2. First, we will draw the **Base Flange** profile. Start a Sketch on the Top Plane and sketch a 350x600mm rectangle, as shown in *Figure 13.1*:

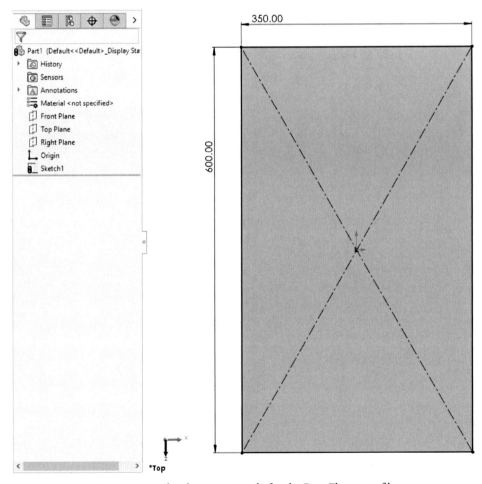

Figure 13.1 – Sketching a rectangle for the Base Flange profile

> **Sketching Tip!**
>
> Remember to always Fully Define your sketches by using Smart Dimensions and Relations.
>
> In this case, I recommend using a **Center Rectangle** tool and starting from the Origin. This will mean that the Front and Right Planes will be at the center of the **Base Flange**. This can be very useful for adding Mates in *assemblies* and also for using **Mirror** features within the *part*.

3.   From within the rectangle sketch, select the **Base Flange/Tab** option to create the first Sheet Metal feature.

For my example, I set the **Sheet Thickness** property as 2mm and the **Bend Allowance** property as a K-Factor of 0.5.

> **Note**
>
> **Sheet thickness selection**
>
> The thickness of your sheet metal parts will depend on exactly what you need to do, and how they will be manufactured and used. Thinner sheet thicknesses will result in parts that are lighter (and cheaper!) but if you are creating large parts then thin sheets can lack rigidity.
>
> **Bend Allowance selections**
>
> In *Chapter 1, Sheet Metal Basics – Exploring Sheet Metal Properties and Material Selection*, we discussed the different types of Bend Allowance in detail, but if you are unsure which Bend Allowance type to use, then the safest option is usually to set a K-Factor of 0.5.
>
> You may also find it helpful to seek advice directly from your manufacturing partner.

Next, we can build up the enclosure base by adding some walls. We could use a simple **Edge Flange** feature, but in my example, I am going to use a **Miter Flange** feature.

> **The Advantages of Using a Miter Flange Feature**
>
> The **Miter Flange** feature allows you to create more complex flange shapes using only a single feature, instead of using multiple **Edge Flange** features to build the same profile. The **Miter Flange** feature will also automatically miter any corners (trim them to fit together properly), whereas not all **Edge Flange** types will do this.

4. Start a Sketch on the small end face of the **Base Flange** and use the **Line** tool to draw the profile shown in *Figure 13.2*. The vertical line is 75mm long and the small, horizontal line is 10mm long:

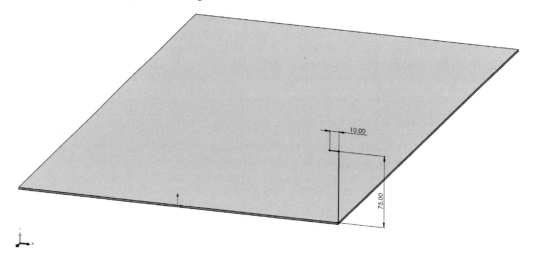

Figure 13.2 – Sketching the Miter Flange profile

5. The sketch profile can now be used to create the flange. Select the **Miter Flange** tool (from within the sketch). Then, select the four edges of the **Base Flange** (*Figure 13.3*):

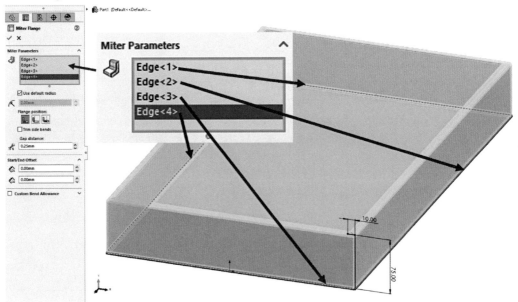

Figure 13.3 – Creating the Miter Flange

Note that the corners of the flanges are mitered so that they fit together properly. The square corners of the flange profile have also been rounded off with the model's Bend Radius.

Setting or Changing the Bend Radius

The default Bend Radius applies to all bends within the Sheet Metal model (unless it is overridden for specific features). The Bend Radius value was set automatically when creating the first Sheet Metal feature, but it can be adjusted by editing the **Sheet-Folder** in the FeatureManager Design Tree.

In practical terms, the Bend Radius depends on a number of factors, primarily the thickness of the sheet being bent (as well as material type and the actual bending process used). Try speaking to your manufacturer or searching online for typical Bend Radius values.

---

6. Set the **Miter Flange** parameters according to your preferences and then press **OK** to create the feature.

    We can now see that we created a simple enclosure base using only two features. If we had used **Edge Flanges**, then more features would have been required to build up the flange shape (especially if we had added more overhangs or other details).

7. **Save** your part by pressing the *Ctrl + S* keys, clicking on the **Save** icon, or by going to **File | Save As….**

Saving in SolidWorks

Try to get into the habit of regularly saving your models, as SolidWorks does occasionally crash during use.

We have now created a simple enclosure base, and in the next section, we will build upon this by adding more features.

Adding more details to the enclosure

Now that we have the bare bones of the enclosure base, we can begin to add some more features to expand the functionality. We will start by adding some circular cut-outs to the front face of the base. These holes might be for LED indicators, for cables, or perhaps even for ventilation.

There are three main ways that we can make circular cut-outs in SolidWorks Sheet Metal:

- **Simple Hole**: This tool allows basic circles to be cut into a sheet. The circle diameter is specified using the tool's Property Manager but this tool is the least useful of the three options because the sketch of the feature then needs editing to specify the exact position of the hole. For this reason, it is often just as fast to use one of the other two options.

- **Extruded Cut**: This option can be used, along with the **Circle** Tool, to make circular holes, but it is more useful when creating non-circular cut-outs. This is shown in more detail when we create a rectangular opening, later in this section.

- **Hole Wizard**: The Hole Wizard is usually the best option for creating circular holes because it allows the exact hole size and type to be specified, either from a range of preset sizes or by using custom parameters. Multiple holes can then be quickly added, and it is very easy to position them and to edit any details at later stages.

Of the three options above, the Hole Wizard tends to be best for creating circular holes, whereas Extruded Cut works best for non-circular cut-outs. The Simple Hole is the least useful option.

Continuing on with the base enclosure model from the previous section, we can now use the Hole Wizard to cut some holes, and then later in the section, we will use Extruded Cut to make a rectangular cut-out:

1. Select the **Hole Wizard** tool. This can be found on the **Features** tab.

2. First, set the hole type and size. There are many options to choose from, but for simple, circular holes, a good option is the **Hole** type (upper-right button – see *Figure 13.4*) and the **Dowel Hole** sub-type (chosen from the drop-down menu). The hole diameter can then be selected from a range of preset sizes, or an exact size can be inputted by putting a check mark in the **Show custom sizing** box and then adding the value.

In this case, I created a hole **20mm** in diameter:

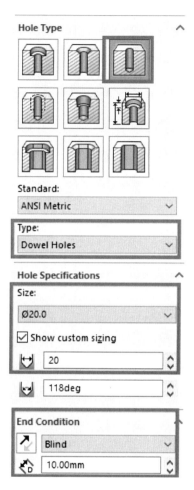

Figure 13.4 – Setting the hole type and size

At this stage, we can also set the **End Condition** as **Blind** with a depth of **10mm**. This will prevent the holes from cutting all the way through both the front and back faces of the enclosure.

3. Now that the hole details are specified, we can set their position. Select the **Position** tab at the top of the Hole Wizard Property Manager then select the face where the holes will be added. In our example, this will be the front face of the enclosure.

    The cursor will change to the **Point** tool and a hole will be placed anywhere a *point* is added. Add two holes to the front face, as shown in *Figure 13.5*:

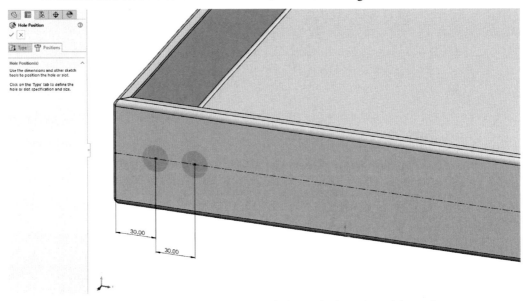

Figure 13.5 – Adding two 20mm diameter holes to the front face of the enclosure

> **Using Centerlines to Line Up Holes**
>
> When using the Hole Wizard (and other sketch-based features) centerlines can be extremely useful. In the example shown in *Figure 13.5*, a centerline was added between the two midpoints of the vertical edges of the front face. In this way, the holes can be lined up along the vertical center of the face.

4. Use Smart Dimensions, Relations, and centerlines (if needed) to Fully Define the hole positions, and then press **OK** to add the holes.

Design Intent When Dimensioning, and Placing Holes Close to Edges and Bends

When dimensioning items in SolidWorks, try to always consider your design intent. For example, in *Figure 13.6*, consider how we could dimension the two holes.

If both holes are dimensioned from the left-hand edge of the enclosure (*Figure 13.6* – left) and then the position of the first hole changed, then the position of the second one would be unaffected.

However, if the holes are dimensioned relative to each other (*Figure 13.6* – right) and then the position of the first hole changed, then the second hole would also move.

The exact way you dimension your features and sketches will depend on your design requirements, but try to keep this in mind when modeling.

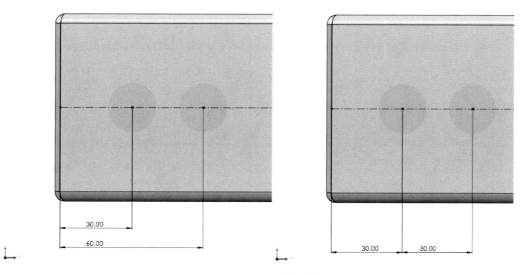

Figure 13.6 – Design intent when dimensioning

5. With the first two holes added, now we can create a rectangular cut-out. This might be used to house something like a USB port. When making these non-circular shapes, it is usually best to use the **Extruded Cut** option.

    First, start a sketch on the front face, and then draw the cut-out profile, as shown in *Figure 13.7*.

This was made using **Center Rectangle** and **Sketch Fillets** to round the corners. Again, centerlines can be useful for lining the sketch entities up with other elements such as the two holes.

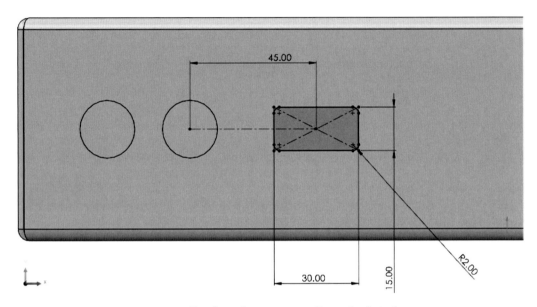

Figure 13.7 – Sketching the cut-out profile on the front face

Using External References

If you are creating a design that uses pre-existing components, then it can be useful to create a SolidWorks *assembly* containing all of the *parts* and then to edit the new *parts* within the *assembly*.

For example, if this enclosure design had a PCB model that was associated with it, then we could create an *assembly* containing both the enclosure and the PCB files. We could then edit the enclosure *part*, *within the assembly*, and use the PCB *part* to line up any cut-outs or other details. This would mean that if the PCB *part* later changed, then the enclosure *part* would automatically update to match these changes.

6. We can now use the rounded rectangle profile to create the cut-out. From within the sketch, select the **Extruded Cut** tool.

Select the **Link to thickness** option in the Property Manager. This will mean that the profile will only be cut through the selected face.

7. Press **OK** to create the cut-out (*Figure 13.8*):

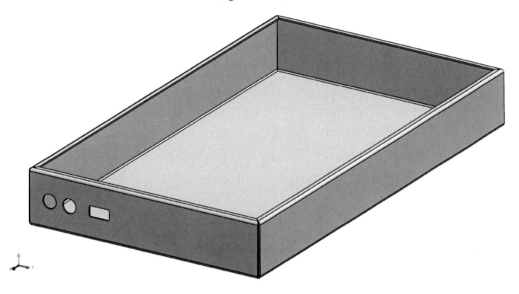

Figure 13.8 – The rectangular cut-out next to the two holes

Often with sheet metal designs, you will find that identical features are repeated throughout the model. Because of this, the **Mirroring** and **Patterning** features can be used to save time.

In this case, we can mirror the cut-outs over on the other side of the enclosure.

8. Select the **Mirror** tool from the **Features** tab, and then select both the **Hole Wizard** feature (the two circular holes) and the **Extruded Cut** (the rectangular cut-out). The **Mirror Plane** will be the large plane down the center of the model (this should be the Right Plane).

Press **OK** to add the mirrored features (*Figure 13.9*):

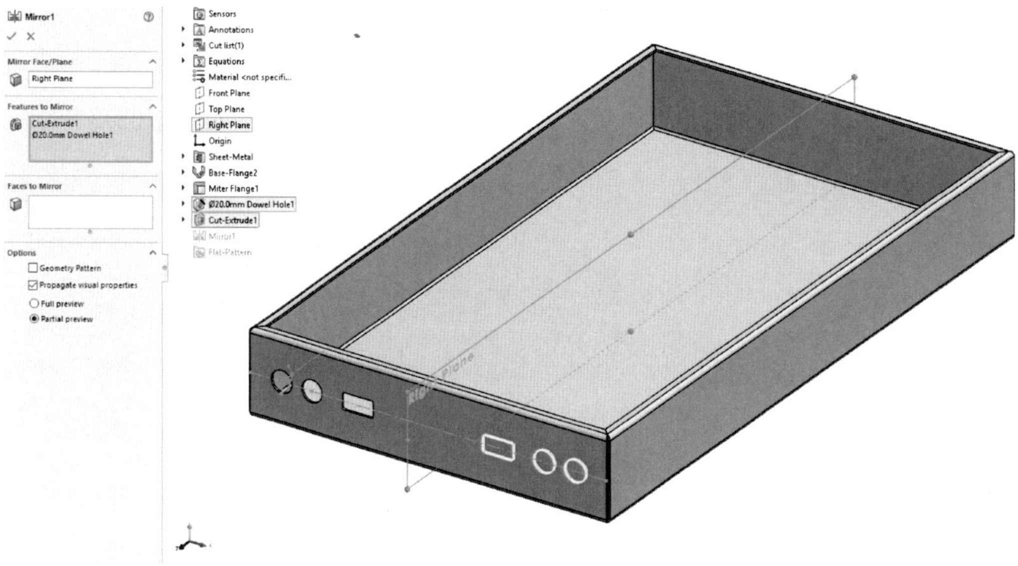

Figure 13.9 – Mirroring the cut-outs

9. Note that we could have also used a **Linear Pattern** if we wanted to add more instances, spaced along the front face.

We have now added a few more details to the base section of the enclosure in the form of both circular and rectangular openings. In the next section, we will create the lid, before returning to the base to add some final finishing touches.

Creating an enclosure lid

Next, we are going to add a new **Base Flange** to the model to create the enclosure's lid. This will turn the model into a multi-sheet *part*.

To add the lid, follow these steps:

1. First, we need to draw a profile for the new **Base Flange**. Start a sketch on the small upper face of the existing **Miter Flange** walls. Then use a **Corner Rectangle** to draw a rectangle that is slightly larger than the existing enclosure base all the way around (*Figure 13.10*):

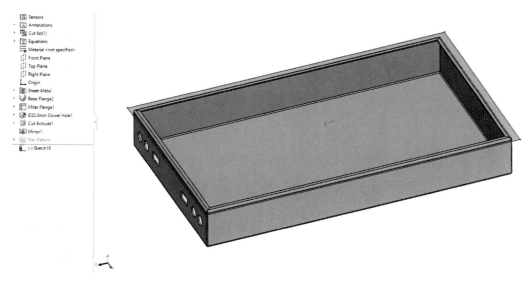

Figure 13.10 – Sketching a Corner Rectangle on the small upper face of the Miter Flange walls

2. Now, we can fix the sides of the rectangle to the sides of the base using Relations. This method takes slightly longer than just using a **Center Rectangle** and setting a size using Smart Dimension, but it means that if the size of the base changes later, the size of the lid will automatically update to match this.

    In turn, select one of the sides of the sketched rectangle, and then also select the corresponding side of the base underneath (hold down the *Ctrl* key in order to select multiple items. Note that this is much easier from a Top view).

Then, make the two selected items Collinear. This can be done by selecting **Make Collinear** from the small popup menu (*Figure 13.11*), or by choosing **Collinear** from the **Add Relations** section of the Property Manager on the left:

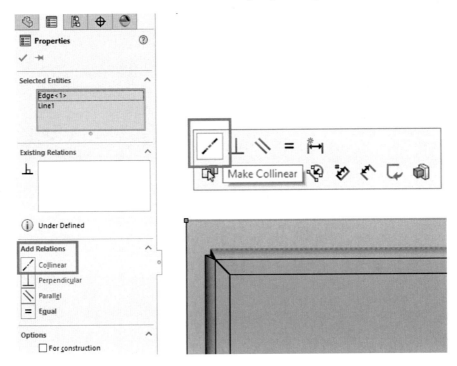

Figure 13.11 – Making the sides of the sketched rectangle Collinear with the existing base

3. Continue the process with the remaining three edges so that the entire rectangle is Fully Defined and linked to the base section underneath (*Figure 13.12*):

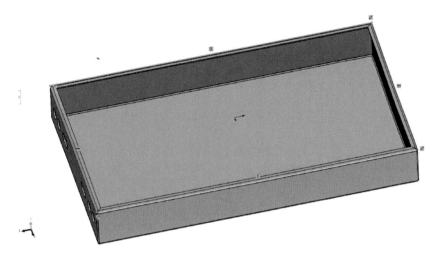

Figure 13.12 – Linking to the rectangle sketch to the base

4. We can now use the Fully Defined rectangle to create the lid sheet.

    Select the **Base Flange/Tab** tool. Then, before pressing **OK**, uncheck the **Merge Result** box. This will mean that the new **Base Flange** will be created as an entirely new sheet within the *part*, instead of being merged with the existing base sheet.

    It may also be necessary for you to flip the direction of the new **Base Flange** to ensure that it doesn't clash with the existing base features (*Figure 13.13*). This can be done by clicking the **Reverse direction** box:

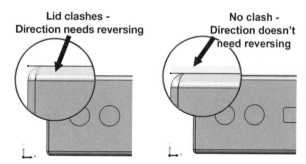

Figure 13.13 – Reverse the direction of the lid flange, if needed

5. Press **OK** to create the lid sheet. We can now see that the **Cut list** folder in the FeatureManager Design Tree (*Figure 13.14*) shows two different sheets – one for the base and one for the lid. If we expand the folder, we can show or hide each of the sheets in turn.

    Note that if your **Cut list** folder shows one single sheet, then try editing the latest **Base Flange/Tab** feature and ensuring that the **Merge result** option is deselected:

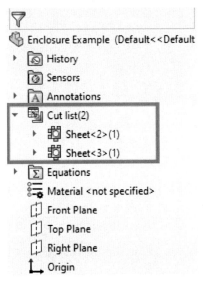

Figure 13.14 – The Cut list folder, showing both sheets

6. We can now see that the basic lid feature has been made, but at the moment, it just consists of a single, flat sheet. It is likely (depending on the thickness) that this sheet would flex under load and would lack rigidity. It would also slide around on the upper surface of the base section. To solve these two issues, we can add some small, overhanging sides to the lid:

    I.   Select the **Edge Flange** tool and use it to add flanges to the short, front edge and the two longer side edges (*Figure 13.15*). These flanges can be 1 0mm long, with a 9 0° angle.

    II. Select the Material Outside flange position to ensure that the new Edge Flanges are clear of the base sheet:

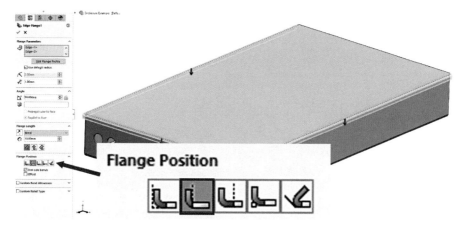

Figure 13.15 – Add three Edge Flanges to the lid

7. Press **OK** to create the three **Edge Flanges**. Note that we haven't added a flange to the rear edge. This is because in real life, the lid could be attached to the base using a long piano hinge (*Figure 13.16*):

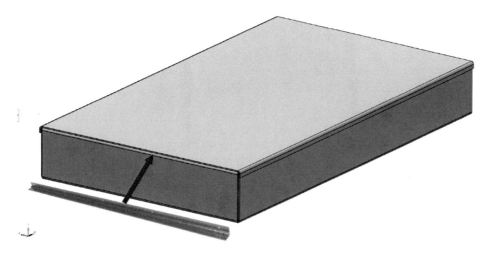

Figure 13.16 – An example piano hinge for joining the lid to the base

8. The rear corners of the new **Edge Flanges** are still square and could be quite sharp, so use the **Break Corner/Corner Trim** options to round these off with a 5mm fillet (*Figure 13.17*):

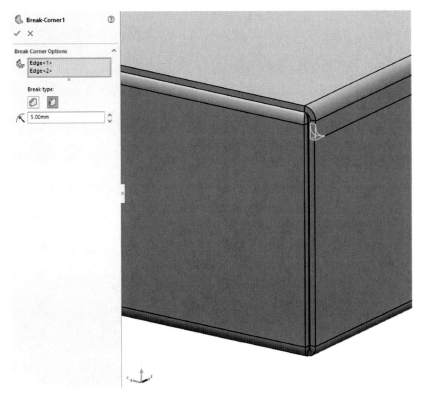

Figure 13.17 – Breaking the rear corners using a 5mm fillet

Now, we have a fairly simple base and lid, but if we look closely at how the two sheets fit together, we may potentially see an issue. The lid currently fits *exactly* on the base, with no clearance (*Figure 13.18*). They are both the same size:

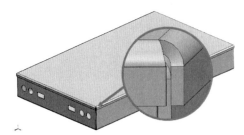

Figure 13.18 – There is no clearance between the lid and the base

This could cause a problem because, in real life, parts are never made exactly the same size as they are modeled in SolidWorks. They will always be slightly larger or smaller, due to manufacturing limitations. This difference between the size of designed parts and the size of the manufactured parts is known as **tolerance**.

For example, a *10mm* long part may be specified as *10.0±1mm*. This would give a real-life part between the size of *9.0mm* and *11.0mm*.

Tolerances can be reduced (although tighter tolerances will result in increased manufacturing costs), but they will never be completely eliminated. Therefore, we should always design clearance between two parts that should fit together (unless we want an extremely tight interference fit as part of our design).

For our example, this means that we should leave a gap between the lid and base sheets. This means that if the lid is made below tolerance (slightly smaller than the SolidWorks model) and the base is made slightly above tolerance (a little larger than the SolidWorks model), then the two sheets will still fit together.

To add this clearance, we can simply edit the **Edge Flanges** and move them outward:

1. Edit the **Edge Flange** feature and select the **Offset** option from the **Flange Position** section. The exact clearance amount depends on the tolerances – set by your budget, manufacturing processes, and your design requirements – but in this example, input a value of 0 . 5mm (*Figure 13.19*):

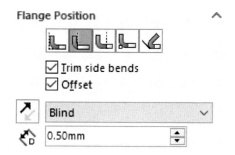

Figure 13.19 – Offsetting the Edge Flanges on the lid

2. To finish off the lid, we will now also add a **Hem** to the inside of the lid. This will prevent users from handling the sharp lower edges of the lid flanges.

    Select the **Hem** tool, and then add a **Closed Hem**, 5mm long, to the inside edges of the three **Edge Flanges** (*Figure 13.20*):

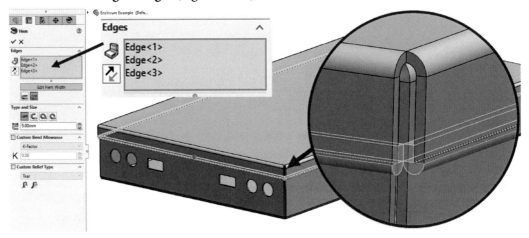

Figure 13.20 – Adding Hems to the three Edge Flanges on the lid

3. The extra thickness added by the **Hems** now means that the lid clashes with the base (this can be checked with the **Interference Detection** tool – see the following note). To fix this, edit the **Edge Flanges** again and increase the **Offset** value to 2 . 6mm to account for the extra folded over material of the **Hems**.

Interference Detection Tool

The **Interference Detection** tool can be found on the **Evaluate** tab and is an extremely useful feature of SolidWorks. It can be used within both *parts* and *assemblies* to check whether the model has any areas that clash with each other.

To use it, select the tool, and then choose the desired bodies, sheets, or *parts*, and press **Calculate**. Any interferences between the different areas will be shown in red.

---

4. A final check of the lid may reveal that the **Hems** corners clash (this will depend on your **Edge Flange Gap** settings).

    If you find that these areas do clash with each other (*Figure 13.21*), then edit the **Edge Flange** feature and increase the **Gap distance**.

In my case, **3mm** was a sufficient gap. Note that these clashes may not be picked up by the **Interference Detection** tool, as they are within one single sheet, not between different sheets, bodies, or *parts*:

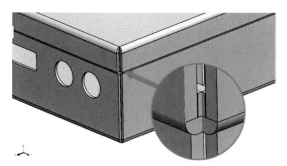

Figure 13.21 – Increasing the Edge Flange Gap distance to avoid the Hem corners clashing

The lid sheet is now completed and, if necessary, we can use the **Flatten** tool to flatten it to check that everything looks correct.

Flattening Sheets in Multi-Sheet Models

When using the **Flatten** tool to check models, only one single sheet can be flattened at any one time.

To select which sheet should be flattened, first expand the **Flat-pattern** folder at the end of the FeatureManager Design Tree. There will be one **Flat-Pattern** feature for each sheet in the model. Select the required sheet and then click **Flatten**. The selected sheets will be flattened and all other sheets will disappear from view.

Press the **Flatten** button again to unflatten the sheet and the rest of the model will reappear.

We have now created a simple enclosure base and a corresponding lid. In the next section, we will add some finishing touches to the enclosure.

Adding final details to the enclosure

Now that we have a basic enclosure design, we can finish it off by adding some rear ventilation and by using **Forming Tools** to add some handles to the front face. This enclosure is a fairly simple example, but it shows the process that could be followed to build more complex designs by using simple steps.

First, we will add some ventilation to the rear face of the enclosure using the **Vent** tool. We could also cut these vents manually, but the **Vent** tool speeds up this process:

1. All **Vents** require a sketch of the **Vent** layout, so start a sketch on the rear face of the enclosure and draw the profile shown in *Figure 13.22*.

2. A centerline was used to find the vertical midpoint of the rear face, and then the **Circle** tool and **Offset Entities** were used to add the three circles. The **Line** tool and **Circular Sketch Pattern** tool were used to add the five Ribs.

    The outer circle is 40mm in diameter, with two smaller circles, each one offset inwards by 8mm. The circles are 140mm from the Origin, which is at the center of the rear face:

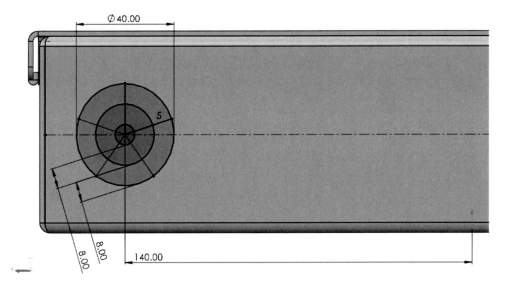

Figure 13.22 – Sketching the Vent details on the rear face

Creating Features Close to Sheet Edges and Bends

Be aware that some manufacturers may have limits on how close cut-outs and other features can be made to sheet edges and bends. If your features are within *10mm* (approximately 0.40") of an edge or bend, it is worth checking any production limitations with your manufacturer.

---

3. We can now start creating the **Vent** feature. Select the **Vent** tool and use the sketch to populate the fields in the Property Manager. I used the following parameters (*Figure 13.23*):

- **Boundary**: Select the outer (40mm) circle.

- **Ribs**: Select the five straight lines. The ribs are 2mm thick.

- **Spars**: Select the middle (32mm) circle. The spars are 2mm thick.

- **Fill In Area**: Select the smallest (24mm) circle.

- **Set a 2mm radius**: This will round off all of the sharp internal corners of the vent:

Figure 13.23 – Creating the Vent

4. Press **OK** to create the **Vent**. Even though we have only made one vent, we can now add more of these by patterning them.

5. Select **Linear Pattern** (from the **Features** tab).

   Use the **Vent** feature that we just created and set a spacing value of 70mm, five instances, and select one of the edges along the top or bottom of the rear face as the pattern direction (*Figure 13.24*).

Figure 13.24 – Patterning the Vent using a Linear Pattern

6. Finally, we can add some formed handles to finish off the design.

   Open the **Design Library** pane on the right-hand side of the screen and navigate to the `forming tools` folder. Then, find the `louvers` subfolder. This folder should contain a louver Forming Tool (*Figure 13.25*).

> **Note**
>
> If you are unable to find the louver tool, then you can create a custom forming tool, as detailed in *Chapter 10, Adding 3D Details to Models with Forming Tools*:

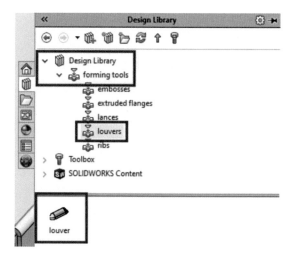

Figure 13.25 – Finding the louver Forming Tool

Left-click and drag the louver Forming Tool onto the front face of the base to add the formed louver shape to that face.

7. Use the **Positions** tab within the Forming Tool Property Manager to precisely position the Forming Tool (*Figure 13.26*). You may have to use the **Point** tool to place a *point* at the position where the tool should be placed:

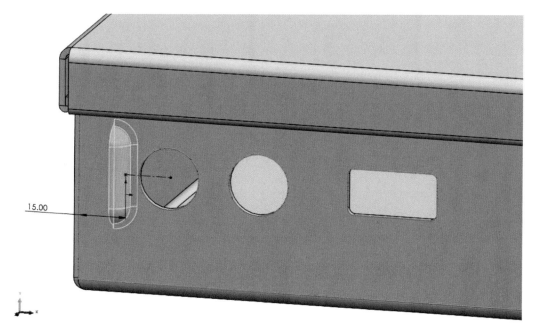

Figure 13.26 – Positioning the formed handle

8. Press **OK** to add the formed handle feature.

9. We can now see that the circular holes and the formed handles are too close together. Edit the **Hole Wizard** feature and move the two holes further away from the edge of the enclosure (*Figure 13.27*). The rectangular cut-out should also move position automatically since its position is defined relative to the two circular holes:

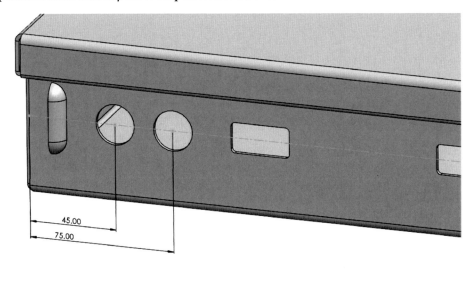

Figure 13.27 – Adjusting the position of the two circular holes (and the associated rectangular cut-out)

10. All that remains is to add a second formed handle to the other side of the front face. Select the **Mirror** tool (from the **Features** tab), and then set the Right Plane as the **Mirror Face/Plane** and the **louver** feature as **Features to mirror** (*Figure 13.28*). Press **OK** to add the second handle.

These two louvers could now be used as handles to pull the tray out from a server cabinet:

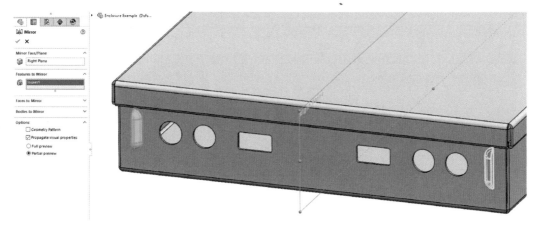

Figure 13.28 – Mirroring the formed handles

This is how our completed sheet metal enclosure looks:

Figure 13.29 – The completed sheet metal enclosure

Congratulations – our sheet metal enclosure design is now complete (*Figure 13.29*)! Although this is a reasonably simple design, it has shown how we can use a multitude of different features to build up a model. These individual elements are not complex, but taken together, they can be combined to create more advanced designs.

Summary

In this chapter, we combined various techniques that we have learned through the book to create a sheet metal enclosure. The base was made using a **Base Flange**, **Miter Flange**, and various cut-outs, **Vents**, and **Formed Tools**.

The lid was built from another simple **Base Flange**, with **Edge Flange** sides and **Hems** to make it more user-friendly.

This design drew upon a number of Sheet Metal tools and features, but the range of designs that you can create with the entire suite of SolidWorks Sheet Metal is only limited by your imagination and design requirements.

As with most elements of SolidWorks, the key to mastering Sheet Metal is to practice the techniques wherever possible. Try looking out for sheet metal products in your day-to-day life and then think about how you might model these in SolidWorks.

Sheet Metal is a great addition to the standard SolidWorks set of tools and one that can be used to take your modeling skills to the next level.

Index

Packt.com

Subscribe to our online digital library for full access to over 7,000 books and videos, as well as industry leading tools to help you plan your personal development and advance your career. For more information, please visit our website.

Why subscribe?

- Spend less time learning and more time coding with practical eBooks and Videos from over 4,000 industry professionals

- Improve your learning with Skill Plans built especially for you

- Get a free eBook or video every month

- Fully searchable for easy access to vital information

- Copy and paste, print, and bookmark content

Did you know that Packt offers eBook versions of every book published, with PDF and ePub files available? You can upgrade to the eBook version at packt.com and as a print book customer, you are entitled to a discount on the eBook copy. Get in touch with us at customercare@packtpub.com for more details.

At www.packt.com, you can also read a collection of free technical articles, sign up for a range of free newsletters, and receive exclusive discounts and offers on Packt books and eBooks.

Other Books You May Enjoy

If you enjoyed this book, you may be interested in these other books by Packt:

Learn SOLIDWORKS 2020

Tayseer Almattar

ISBN: 978-1-78980-410-2

- Understand the fundamentals of SOLIDWORKS and parametric modeling.

- Create professional 2D sketches as bases for 3D models using simple and advanced modeling techniques.

- Use SOLIDWORKS drawing tools to generate standard engineering drawings.

- Evaluate mass properties and materials for designing parts and assemblies.

- Understand the objectives and the formats of the CSWA and CSWP exams.

Managing and Visualizing Your BIM Data

Ernesto Pellegrino | Jisell Howe | Manuel André Bottiglieri | Dounia Touil | Luisa Cypriano Pieper

ISBN: 978-1-80107-398-1

- Understand why businesses across the world are moving toward data-driven models.

- Build a data bridge between BIM models and web-based dashboards.

- Get to grips with Autodesk Dynamo with the help of multiple step-by-step exercises.

- Focus on data gathering workflows with Dynamo.

- Connect Power BI to different datasets.

Packt is searching for authors like you

If you're interested in becoming an author for Packt, please visit `authors.packtpub.com` and apply today. We have worked with thousands of developers and tech professionals, just like you, to help them share their insight with the global tech community. You can make a general application, apply for a specific hot topic that we are recruiting an author for, or submit your own idea.

Hi!

I'm Johno Ellison, author of *Mastering SOLIDWORKS Sheet Metal*. I really hope you enjoyed reading this book and found it useful for improving your SolidWorks skills.

It would really help me (and other potential readers!) if you could leave a review on Amazon sharing your thoughts on *Mastering SOLIDWORKS Sheet Metal*.

Go to the link below or scan the QR code to leave your review:

https://packt.link/r/1803245247

Your review will help me to understand what's worked well in this book, and what could be improved upon for future editions, so it really is appreciated.

Best Wishes,

Made in the USA
Las Vegas, NV
19 October 2024

10071747R00181